Educational Theory
As
Theory of Conduct _____

Educational Theory As Theory of Conduct

From Aristotle to Dewey

J.J. Chambliss

State University of New York Press

Published by
State University of New York Press, Albany

For information, address State University of New York Press, State University Plaza, Albany, N.Y., 12246

Library of Congress Cataloging-in-Publication Data

Chambliss, J.J. (Joseph James), 1929-
  Educational theory as theory of conduct.

  Bibliography: p.
  Includes index.
  1. Education—Philosophy—History. 2. Education—
Aims and objectives. 3. Conduct of life. I. Title.
LB41.C49   1987   370'.1   86-14540
ISBN 0-88706-463-9
ISBN 0-88706-464-7 (pbk.)

10   9   8   7   6   5   4   3   2   1

170290

CONTENTS _____

PREFACE

This essay is in no sense an attempt to provide a comprehensive history of educational theory from Aristotle to Dewey. Its aim is a more modest one, to show the nature of an idea that has endured in that history. The idea that educational theory is a theory of conduct is one from which we cannot escape. Yet we neglect it all too often. We ignore it when we try to direct education into paths laid out by measures that quantify conduct, or when we use Graduate Record Examination scores as a device to determine who should be educated. Just because conduct is made of certainty and uncertainty, of rationality and irrationality, of the measured and the immeasurable, it resists efforts to settle its nature in terms of the certain, measured, and rational. The certain, the measured, the rational are dimensions of conduct which educate us, but they are not the only ones; the uncertain, the irrational, and the immeasurable educate us also. Each dimension has its limitations and its possibilities and needs to be taken into account in determining what we do in educating ourselves. The idea that educational theory is a theory of conduct is an argument against scientism in its various forms. Conduct, like love, must *find* its ways despite the efforts of scientism to computerize it or to fix the stages through which it passes.

My chief intellectual debts are to the writers whose ideas make up the subject matter of the essay. There are other debts to acknowledge, some of an intellectual kind, and some that are more personal. An enormous debt is owed to students in the course "Educational Classics," where the ideas in this essay have been presented, developed, tolerated, and discussed. My friend and colleague, James M. Giarelli, has been a sympathetic listener to the idea that educational theory is a theory of conduct. Margaret Nolan helped in the typing of an earlier draft. Sandra Chubrick typed the present version. And Marie Bograd knows that she had a special part in it.

The material in two chapters follows closely articles already published. My gratitude is to the editors of their respective journals for permission to include the following: "Oratory as Conduct in Cicero and Quintilian," *Journal of the Midwest History of Education Society,* XIV (1986), 68–78, is Chapter IV; and "The Educational Significance of 'Nature' and 'Conduct' in Condillac's Logic," *Paedagogica Historica,* XVII (June, 1977), 50–61, is Chapter X.

equations. In another sense, students learn to bring paintings, sculptures, poetry into existence. In yet another sense, students working together bring into existence a shared responsibility for their actions. Each sense is an example of conduct; conduct is action; and to act is to do. Each example of conduct is a way of educating.

The idea that ways of thinking about education are ways of thinking about conduct is the point of departure for the present essay. As we have seen in the examples of terms defined in the *Oxford English Dictionary,* the idea points to something so familiar in our experience that it seems almost unnecessary to discuss it. It is clear that it would be difficult to find anything about either education or conduct that would enable us to deny the truth of the idea that educational theory is a theory of conduct. Even so, being familiar with an idea is one thing; knowing it is another. As Hegel wrote, "What is familiar is not known simply because it is familiar."[4] For this reason we need to discuss the idea.

In the history of ideas that have shaped educational theory, two traditions have endured from classical antiquity to the present time. In one tradition, we find the tendency to write of education and conduct in ways such that theories of education are theories *about* conduct. Thinkers who stand in this tradition hold that principles of conduct exist in the nature of things, and the aim of educational theory is to know the principles. Once they are known, however, principles stand apart from human conduct and are held to determine conduct. Principles are taken to be the standards for which human beings exist, and take on an existence of their own apart from conduct. There is no single source of principles in this tradition. Three sources, however, stand out. (1) One source is reason. Geometry, with its axioms and postulates as unprovable premises of proof, has served as a standard against which all thinking may be judged. If only the human mind could come to understand a rational system of conduct with axioms and postulates of its own, then human conduct might be shaped as are theorems in geometry. The idea has taken various forms in the thinking of Descartes, Spinoza, Locke, and others. (2) There are otherworldly sources of principles of conduct, where the source is literally beyond and superior to human experience, and thus capable of evaluating it. For example, believers in otherworldly standards set forth in the word of God hold that they have no need of human conduct. Again the standards for human conduct stand apart from that conduct. (3) Another source is science, not primarily rational as geometry is, but an inductive one whose principles are derived from experience. Some advocates of this conception of science treat its principles as if they are about conduct rather than *of* conduct. For example, certain attempts to develop a science of human development first hold that development takes place by stages, then treat the stages as if they are principles which determine human conduct. In each source, whether "rational," "otherworldly," or "scientific," there is a tendency to treat principles as if they are entitled to determine and judge actual conduct.

In the second tradition, writers have worked on theories of education in which the nature of conduct has to be worked out in experience. These thinkers have recognized what John Locke called the "various and unknown humours, interests, and capacities of men,"[5] and what John Dewey called the "unreconciled diversity" and the "recalcitrant particular"[6] in reality. The nature of experience that is worked out in this tradition is an empirical matter, not a nature that can be known in advance of the actual experience. This is a way of saying that theories of education must be theories *of* conduct, rather than theories *about* conduct. Thus theories themselves must be shaped in conduct, not apart from it. Only by trying to make principles of conduct may human beings understand them. The present essay emphasizes the second tradition. Yet something of the first tradition enters into our account, for not all the writers we consider stand unequivocally in the second tradition. Some of them are of two minds, as we shall see.

We begin with Aristotle's predecessors, and discuss the ideals of conduct celebrated in Homer's *Iliad*, the poetry of Sappho, tragic poetry, and Pindar's odes. We continue with Isocrates' orator and Plato's philosopher. These writings show us something of the conceptions of conduct in which Aristotle's ideas took shape. His *Nicomachean Ethics* and *Politics* stand as the turning point in our study of conduct. This is so because Aristotle's work is a criticism and a culmination of the ideas on conduct which preceded him and made his own work possible. And, what is just as important, the conceptions of conduct which followed him owe much to his thinking. After Aristotle we consider Cicero and Quintilian, who argue that oratory is an art whose nature is action. Educated in right conduct, the meaning of an orator's life is expressed in his orations. The place of conduct is evident also in the writings of Philo of Alexandria and two ancient Christians, Clement of Alexandria and Augustine. For Philo, studies in classic poetry and philosophy are the beginning of wisdom, preparatory to the true wisdom found in Jewish religious literature. In Clement's view, because the classical studies teach us a worldly wisdom from which we need to escape, the innocence of childhood is the kind of conduct which adults should imitate. Augustine holds that Christians must conduct themselves in certain ways, as characterized by his "seven steps to Wisdom," if they are to attain the highest end possible for human nature.

In turning to *The Metalogicon* of John of Salisbury, we see a Christian defense of the ancient arts of poetry, oratory, and philosophy. The aim is not to study these arts for their own sake, but for the examples of human conduct expressed in them. Put differently, it is for the sake of doing "good works" that we study the arts. John Locke, the first of the moderns whom we consider, argues that it is possible to construct a demonstrative science of ethics. Yet the feature of his writings which captures our attention is the place given to the wisdom in common sense, and to the probabilistic character of human conduct. Walking in Locke's footsteps, Isaac Watts emphasizes the sense in which logic is a kind of action. Giambattista Vico's writings echo the ancient wisdom which seeks likely or probable explanations for action. The idea that human beings have made themselves as social beings and, therefore, can understand themselves, stimulates him to write a "new science" of human conduct. Rousseau's fascination with the possibility of understanding human beings in their original, "natural" state, led him to write hypothetical accounts of human beings in developing their social nature. In the works of Rousseau's imagination, it is human conduct that shapes our social nature. Rousseau's contemporary, Condillac, writes a *Logic* in which he argues that we may learn to conduct ourselves in a logical way if we follow the lessons which nature gives. Logic is better understood as an artful way of conduct than as a set of rules which are to govern conduct. Our story ends with John Dewey, who holds that the nature of the good is determined in the experience of living as a social being, not by principles that transcend experience.

While our thinkers hold in common the idea that theory of education is a theory of conduct, we will see that (1) they are not in complete agreement as to their theories of education or conduct, and (2) some of them appear to be of two minds. What they do share in common is a keen sense that matters of morality are inescapably matters of conduct and that in such matters the essence of education is to be found. This is so even where there is essential disagreement about the nature of the conduct that is desired, as, for example, between a naturalist such as Aristotle and a Christian such as Augustine.

Those, as Plato and Locke, who appear to be of two minds, show us tension between the idea that morality is a matter of conduct, and the idea that we may know principles which determine the nature of conduct. Desiring a rationalistic science of conduct, they remain sensitive to the "recalcitrant particulars" in conduct. Yet these writers do not show us any principles of conduct, despite yearning to know them. Like the other thinkers we discuss, they do not forsake the search for practical wisdom in conduct by substituting for it the quest for certainty.

Aristotle's statement that, "in doing, the end cannot be other than the act itself,"[7] points to the essential idea that is common to the theories of conduct that we will discuss. We conclude with Dewey, whose characterization of growth as *being* an end rather than *having* an end[8] is true to

Aristotle's idea. We will see that some of our thinkers are tempted by the quest for certainty. Even so, from Aristotle to Dewey one idea endures: We must settle for the probable, the uncertain, the incomplete, as inescapable conditions of conduct.

The main sources of ideas for this study are the writers whose ideas we discuss. Yet there is one work which should receive special attention in introducing ours because of its value to students of human conduct. That is Michael Oakeshott's book, *On Human Conduct*.[9] The first part deals with theorizing human conduct; there we are attracted to his claim that to recognize what he calls "a 'going-on' as 'conduct' is to acknowledge it to be something that has had to be learned."[10] To recognize that movements of water or motions caused by the wind are not learned is to say that they are not actions, or conduct. It is to insist, along with our writers, that actions making up conduct are learned. Or we may say that conduct is a kind of learning and must be treated as a matter of education. As a theorist of conduct, Oakeshott is interested in making theories, not in performing actions; he "is concerned with theorems about conduct."[11] At the same time, Oakeshott joins in our insistence that "If . . . doing is recognized as itself an engagement to understand, surely it must be no less the case that every engagement to understand is to be recognized as a 'doing'."[12] After theorizing human conduct, Oakeshott treats civil association (what he calls "an ideal mode of human relationship"), and then examines the character of a modern European state as a kind of human relationship.[13] Thus he (1) theorizes human conduct, (2) treats an ideal human relationship in the light of his theorizing, and (3) considers an actual, or empirical situation involving human relationships.

We agree with Oakeshott that there are certain features of human existence to which we cannot help subjecting ourselves, and that we need to acknowledge this and understand what the features are if conduct is to be made meaningful. To make conduct meaningful is to learn, to educate ourselves. Yet our essay has a different aim from Oakeshott's. We take an idea that is truistic, viz., educational theory is a theory of conduct (rather than a theory of something that is not conduct), and attempt to convince the reader that we cannot escape from the idea. In the terms of Hegel's distinction, we need to "know" the idea, rather than merely be "familiar" with it. Oakeshott takes that idea as a given, and by theorizing, works out the terms of a theory of conduct. The terms are the conditions which constitute a theory of conduct. Our discussion is preliminary to the development of a theory, however, rather than the development of a theory itself. We aim to show that educational theory is a theory of conduct, not to work out the particular terms of a theory of education or of conduct. Of course, our writers consider particular conditions and take into account various terms that are necessary if there is to be any meaningful theory of education; but these conditions and terms do not constitute a theory. To learn that we must settle for probable, uncertain, and incomplete conditions in human conduct is to come to terms with what is necessary in human existence if educational theories true to the nature of human conduct are to be worked out.

Chapter 2

ARISTOTLE'S PREDECESSORS

The question, how is virtue acquired, had been addressed by poets, orators, and philosophers long before Aristotle. He summarizes the positions taken which had long been a part of the conventional wisdom by his time: "Now some thinkers hold that virtue is a gift of nature; others think we become good by habit, others that we can be taught to be good."[1] In large part, however, the idea that some are born with virtue was celebrated in legend rather than found actualized among mortals. One favorite story was of Herakles, who was born already possessing the courage and strength of a full-grown hero. Pindar's account of the infant Herakles goes as follows:

> I follow now with glad heart Herakles, great in the high places of valor. I raise again an ancient story how, at the moment when that child of Zeus escaped the darkness of labor and came with his twin brother forth from his mother's loins into the brightness, he came not unmarked by Hera of the golden throne, even in his child's wrappings saffron-dyed; but the Queen of the gods in her heart's anger sent two snakes against him straightway. These came through the opened gates into the great inner chamber, raging to grip the children in their swift jaws. But Herakles raised his head upright, and essayed his first battle, with two unescapable hands clutching the throat of either serpent. These, strangling at last, gasped out the breath of life from their terrible bodies.[2]

7

Yet the mortals whom Pindar celebrates in his odes had to struggle to become victorious in their contests; though born favored by nature and nature's gods, they were not heroic at birth. Like Herakles, they were born to be heroic; but unlike him, they needed training and experience to become heroic.

Perhaps the closest approximation to possessing virtue by nature were the child prodigies. Pierre Riché writes that these were the only (real) children in antiquity who were considered to be "worthy of interest"; this is because child prodigies "already thought like old men."[3] Inasmuch as most children were neither legendary heroes nor prodigies, the point of view which prevailed was expressed in the idea that virtue is acquired, not inborn.

Pindar's odes express the conviction that things of greatest worth come only to those who are favored by nature: "We are things of a day. What are we? What are we not? The dream of shadow is man, no more. But when the brightness comes, and God gives it, there is a shining of light on men, and their life is sweet."[4] Yet the few who are fortunate enough to receive nobility from nature must learn to discipline themselves. An inborn noble nature is a necessary, but not a sufficient, condition for bringing the victor's prize, in athletic contests and in life. Pindar writes: "Sharpening one born for great achievement, a man, under God's hand aiding, could drive to gigantic glory."[5] And then he adds, "But without striving, few have won joy of victory to be a light upon their lifetime for all deeds accomplished."[6] The excellence which is possessed only by the well-born, in the beginning, is a gift of nature which stands unfulfilled in the potential hero. To gain honor the potential must be actualized; in the athletic contests whose victors are celebrated in Pindar's odes, we see the actualization given its just due by the poet. It is as if the well-born need an entire lifetime to show their mettle in the contests of actual life or, perhaps we should say, in the contest that *is* life. For Pindar, the athletic contest is one of the competitions of life; each contest is an instance of living. Each is a moment in that life in which the well-born is tested in action. "The end shines through in the testing of actions where excellence is shown, as a boy among boys, a man among men, last among the elders, each part that makes our mortal life,"[7] Pindar writes.

We are put in mind of the remark that Aristotle would make later, that one swallow does not make spring, and of his reminding us that it is difficult to become virtuous, in these words of Pindar: "We should seek out some measure in things gained; too bitter are the pangs of madness after loves that are past attainment."[8] And, "If any mortal keeps in mind the way of truth, he must take with grace whatever the gods give."[9] It is clear that we mortals "take" in two senses. (1) In the one sense from which we cannot escape, which means that we can take only what is given. (2) In another

sense, what is given by the gods is a beginning, not an end; it is a potentiality, not an actuality; it requires us to take it and find out its worth in action.
In the second sense, we try to work out our measure in things, we strive for
the end to shine through by the actions we take. The end can be known
only if we take action; it is unknown prior to acting. We may say that what is
given by the gods cannot be known except by the actions of those who
come to possess it. "Silence of obscurity descends on those who will not
endeavor," Pindar writes, "but even among strivers there may be darkness
of luck before they come to the utmost goal."[10] Thus the victories celebrated in Pindar's odes are examples of virtue actualized. They are first made
possible by favors of the gods, but finally are made actual by strivings of
human beings.

The conduct which Pindar sings about in his poetry is the valor of the
noble hero. What his heroes expressed by their victories in athletic contests were examples of the kind of valor lived in Homer's epics. H. I.
Marrou puts it this way: "In Homer each succeeding generation of antiquity
rediscovered the thing that is absolutely fundamental to this whole aristo-
cratic ethics: the love of glory."[11] The point to emphasize here is that the
valor possessed by one who loves glory is exercised only through a kind of
conduct. To achieve the great deed is literally to live in a certain way. What
the poets do is to immortalize the heroes, by attempting to clothe their
deeds in language that itself will be immortal. By Pindar's time, Homer was
already immortal. Pindar sees himself as striving to stand beside Homer in
glorifying heroic virtue: "I will work out the divinity that is busy within my
mind and tend the means that are mine. . . . In the glory of poetry achievement of men blossoms long; but to do this well is given to few."[12] As nature
gives to few men the gifts necessary to act heroically, so to few poets is
given the gift necessary to become great in their craft.

Only the greatest poets can sing the praises of heroes with excellence. As he praises one victor, Pindar hopes that it will be his fortune to
stand beside him: "Let it be yours to walk in this time on the heights. Let it
be mine each time to stand beside you in victory, for my skill at the
forefront of the Hellenes."[13] While the band of potential heroes is a small
one, and the list of poets skilled in ways to celebrate their heroism is short,
most human beings are incapable either of heroism or of understanding
what the best poets say: "There are many sharp shafts in the quiver under
my arm. They speak to the understanding; for most men, they need inter-
preters."[14] In the following passage, Pindar is more exuberant than usual
about what nature is capable of giving, going so far as to say that wisdom
comes by nature: "The wise man knows many things by nature; the vulgar
are taught. They will say anything. They chatter vainly like crows against the
divine bird of Zeus."[15]

Pindar has no compliment for the many, who must be taught. For them, the great deed will not come; not only do they chatter in vain, but they also strive in vain. And practice cannot gain victory for them: "Best by nature is best; but many have striven before now to win by talents acquired by teaching the glory. But the thing unblessed by God is none the worse for silence, always."[16] Thus those who lack nature's blessing are incapable of glory; at the same time, their nature cannot be changed: "No thing, neither hot-colored fox or loud lion, may change the nature born in his blood."[17] For the most part, then, Pindar joins in song with the poets of old, singing of the ways in which the valorous heroes of myth and athletic contest were taught. He writes in praise of the centaur Cheiron, teacher of Achilles and other great men. As a boy, Achilles performed manlike deeds of heroic stature, under Cheiron's direction. Here is Pindar's account:

> Tawny Achilles lived in the house of Philyra and as yet a boy at play did great things; in his hands hefting the javelin scantily tipped with iron, wind-light, he wreaked death in bloody combat upon wild lions; he struck down boars, and to the house of the Kronian centaur dragged the gasping carcasses, at six years, and thereafter for the rest of his time; and amazed Artemis and bold Athene, killing deer without hounds or treacherous nets, for he ran them down in his speed.[18]

In the *Iliad*, Achilles' human tutor, Phoenix—by now an old man—is taken along as part of a deputation which attempted to convince the stubborn Achilles to help his countrymen. Phoenix reminded Achilles that he had been made Achilles' guardian by Peleus when "You were a mere lad, with no experience of the hazards of war, nor of debate, where people make their work. It was to teach you all these things, to make a speaker of you and a man of action, that he sent me to you."[19] In the course of his appeal, Phoenix says, "All my loving devotion has gone to make you what you are."[20] To make one a speaker *and* a man of action; in this are joined the two essential characteristics of Homer's heroes. We see a forerunner here of two ideals: (1) orator as the good man speaking well; and (2) Aristotle's poliscraftsman who articulates the end of action at the beginning of his investigation and then strives to act so as to realize the end which he articulates.

In the spoken word the deed is articulated, imagined, celebrated, or foreshadowed. This is so in Homer's epics, again in Pindar's odes, then in Isocrates' oratory which rivaled poetry as a form of literature by taking itself to be an expression of the ideal of noble conduct. "We do not think that there is an incompatibility between words and deeds," Pericles said in his oration honoring the Athenians who had died in combat; "the worst thing is to rush into action before the consequences have been properly debated."[21] In philosophy we see the self-conscious attempt to examine poetry and oratory in a critical way, and then to put itself forth as their rival. The accounts of heroic conduct in the songs of Homer and Pindar, contests both of word and deed, foreshadow the statements about conduct in oratory and philosophy, where ideals of conduct are set forth in words that require deeds for their fulfillment. In each form of expression we find the continuing concern about human conduct, whether told as fabulous accounts by Homer's heroes, glorified in Pindar's odes and Sappho's lyrics, dramatized in tragic poetry, argued in Isocrates' orations, or sought as the highest human activity in Plato's dialogues and Aristotle's treatises. What H.I. Marrou has said of poetry may be said also of oratory and philosophy, each in its own way: "The poet's function is to educate, and education means inculcating this ideal of glory. The aim of poetry is not essentially aesthetic but the immortalization of the hero."[22]

The persuasive power of oratory is aimed at convincing people to do this or that, to act in certain ways to realize the best prospects of their nature; and while an oration is an art form of a certain kind, one of its aims is to persuade, which is a way of educating. The analytic, critical investigative powers of philosophy also set forth ends of action for human conduct to realize. Philosophy, too, takes on its own forms and thereby is a kind of art, but its aims, whether analytic, critical, or investigative, are primarily educative.

In tragic poetry the necessity of conduct on the part of the tragic figures is apparent. Yet many of those caught in tragic situations are less than heroic. The necessity of things is a web which captures both heroes and nonheroes, and so the nature of the necessity is what most interests us. The nature and place of conduct in tragedy intrigues us. To put it in the form of a question: What kind of necessity is dramatized in the human actions through which tragedy unfolds?

In Aeschylus' *Agamemnon,* we are told by the chorus:

Zeus, whose will has marked for man

The sole way where wisdom lies;

Ordered one eternal plan:

Man must suffer to be wise. [23]

To find the way Zeus has marked for human beings is no easy task, as Agamemnon learned. As Aeschylus' chorus goes on, Agamemnon "put on the harness of Necessity."[24] He offered his young daughter as a sacrifice in order to appease the gods, so that a storm would lift and enable his ships to sail. Yet in sacrificing his daughter, he brings disaster to himself. "Time may show, But cannot alter, what shall be,"[25] is the ancient wisdom about necessity sung by the chorus. At this point, early in the drama, we know that justice of a kind will be done: we know that Agamemnon the killer will be killed.

One reading of this suggests that there is a kind of necessity which transcends any particular actions; that this is a necessity somehow inherent in the nature of things, which in fact brings particular actions to pass. According to this reading, it is as if tragedy is reified in the nature of things; tragedy is a kind of determiner of Agamemnon's actions. In this way tragedy is that which brings human beings to their necessarily tragic ends. Human action, then, is simply determined as part of the conditions of tragedy. Human action is a determined, rather than a determining, factor in tragedy. Yet there is a different reading. Agamemnon helped determine the tragedy which befell him by the actions he took. The sacrifice of his daughter was an action which he chose to take; he was not *destined* to take it. On this reading, Agamemnon was an active participant in determining "what shall be"; time, indeed, "showed" it; but Agamemnon *did* it.

If we consider the actions of Antigone, we can scarcely doubt that her actions contributed to the tragedy in Sophocles' *Antigone*. And we can say the same for Creon, her antagonist. In the drama, Antigone disobeys a decree of King Creon by giving her brother the sort of burial which she believes is required by the "laws of Heaven." In speaking to Creon, whose decree carried a death penalty for anyone who disobeys it, she tells of her willingness to oppose mere manmade law, even to die for opposing it:

Nor could I think that a decree of yours—

A man—could override the laws of Heaven

Unwritten and unchanging. Not of today

Or yesterday is their authority;

They are eternal; no man saw their birth.

For me to meet this doom is little grief;

But when my mother's son lay dead, had I

Neglected him and left him there unburied,

That would have caused me grief; this causes none.[26]

Thus we have a real clash of beliefs. Antigone has acted on hers, and Creon has acted on his. They are both tragic figures; taking action on their different beliefs, they bring about consequences, some of them beyond their control. The tragedy is theirs, not in the sense that it was brought to pass by a necessity which already existed in the nature of things, but in the sense that in their very actions the issue between them was joined. The joining was a way of conduct. In this conduct they made the tragic conditions and could not escape their consequences.

The ways in which human beings participate in making their own tragedies is shown starkly by Euripides in *Hecuba*. The setting for this play is the Greek camp where the Trojan women are held captive after the fall of Troy; Hecuba is the widow of Priam, who had been king of Troy. The Greek leader, Odysseus, has convinced his fellow Greeks that Polyxena, Hecuba's young daughter, must be sacrificed to honor the memory of Achilles, who had died in battle against the Trojans. Hecuba pleads with Odysseus to spare Polyxena, arguing that the Greek laws apply to slaves as well as to free people. And she says to Odysseus:

> *Let her stay with me. Let her live.* Surely there are dead enough without her death. And everything I lost lives on in her. This one life redeems the rest. She is my comfort, my Troy, my staff, my nurse; she guides me on my way. She is all I have. And you have power, Odysseus, greatness and power. But clutch them gently, use them kindly, for power gives no purchase to the hand, it will not hold, soon perishes, and greatness goes. I know. I too was great but I am nothing now. One day cut down my greatness and my pride.[27]

Her arguments and pleas are of no avail; Polyxena is not to be spared. The clever Odysseus uses every device of sophistic rhetoric to justify his own motives, which are really political. In the name of honor, he will sacrifice an innocent maiden; in the name of courage, he will behave as a coward.

When it is clear to Hecuba that her pleas have failed, she urges Polyxena to beg Odysseus for her life. But Polyxena refuses to do so, and speaks to Odysseus, showing her pride and courage:

> I shall not beg for life. No: I go with you because I must, but most because I wish to die. If I refuse, I prove myself a coward, in love with life. But why should I live? I had a father once, king of Phrygia. And so I started life, a princess of the blood, nourished on lovely hopes to be a bride for kings. . . . And now I am a slave. It is that name of slave, so ugly, so strange, that makes me want to die. Or should I live to be knocked down to a bidder, sold to a master for cash? . . . Never. With eyes still free, I now renounce the light and dedicate myself to death. . . . I am a novice to this life of shame, whose yoke I might endure, but with such pain that I prefer to die than go on living.[28]

Her words moved the chorus-leader to pronounce:

> Nobility of birth is a stamp and seal, conspicuous and sharp. But true nobility allied to birth is a greatness and a glory.[29]

Yet Hecuba, exhausted and suffering from the deceit and dishonor that have taken Polyxena from her, cries out that she is unable to see the greatness and the glory in Polyxena's noble action: "I am proud of you, my child, so very proud, but anguish sticks in this nobility."[30] Polyxena's noble virtue is its own reward; for her, there will be no other. For her mother, who had wanted something different, the sharing of Polyxena's life, there is a crying out against the necessity in things which took Polyxena from her. Even so, the courage displayed in Polyxena's innocence becomes part of the necessity in things which made the tragedy the moment of glory that we remember. *This* is the greatness and the glory celebrated by the chorus-leader.

Euripides tells us that the real stuff of tragedy is in human action, amidst the deceivers, the cowards, and other failures of moral fiber. Odysseus acts, not from necessity, but from the excuse of necessity. And so does Agamemnon, who appears later in the drama and says that he cannot act on Hecuba's behalf because he must yield to the opinion of his army. Their actions make a mockery of necessity. Seeing through the excuses made in the name of necessity, Hecuba responds:

> Then no man on earth is truly free. All are slaves of money or necessity. Public opinion or fear of prosecution forces each one, against his conscience, to conform.[31]

In the actions of men such as Odysseus and Agamemnon, Euripides portrays the mocking of necessity. Yet for all the mockery, the mockers, along with Hecuba and Polyxena, contribute to the tragedy. For all the mockery, the tragedy is real. Thus we understand that each tragedy has its own determinants, including its own cowards as well as its own heroes. Its particular cowardice and courage were lived by its participants, not predetermined in the nature of things.

Though young and inexperienced in the ways of the world, by her noble action Polyxena makes a certain tragedy by the way she lives and dies. By the way she "yields to necessity" she shows us a wisdom beyond her years and makes us yearn for a necessity of a different kind. The actual nobility of Polyxena becomes an ideal to those who, failing to find nobility in their own lives, need art if they are to experience something of it. A deed such as Polyxena's is what sculptors have in mind when they cast a noble act in bronze or marble. Lived nobility is so rare that we make it an example in sculpture lest our ordinary experience be barren of it. Polyxena simply *is* what a sculptor of noble scenes strives to show.

What comes through in the portrayal of tragic women such as Antigone, Hecuba, and Polyxena is that nobility is not the prerogative of men, even in the male-dominated societies inhabited by the ancient Greeks, their neighbors, and their enemies. In their tragedies, we see the ways in which human action is a determiner of tragedy. The women, along with Creon, Odysseus, the Greek soldiers, and the imagined gods they were trying to appease, were not so much the stuff of which tragedies are made. Rather they were the stuff which makes tragedies.

The integrity of women and the place they take in giving shape to the nature of things is expressed differently in the lyrical poetry of Sappho. According to one tradition, her verse was held in such high regard by Plato that he called her the tenth Muse. Whether or not there is truth in the tradition, there is truth in the claims which assign to Sappho a unique place among the band of ancient poets. In the two complete poems and the fragments which remain, we are held captive by the idea that conduct is a prerequisite for articulating ideals. The passion, the love, the yearning, which are the subject matter of the poems, are expressions of Sappho's experienced reality and its ideals. She makes us yearn for the courage to have such experience for ourselves, and to tell others about it, if we had her poet's gift to do so.

Sappho's verse gives voice to a kind of intimacy whose yearning is so pure that to touch it would do violence to it. Yet the reader is compelled to want to share in such intimacy. Her verse is articulated in such vivid imagery that it is more like a painting than a poem; or more like sculpture than verse. Yet it is sculpture and painting not silent but alive with passion, with love for the unattained, with seeking that will never find its heart's desire. When she writes, "it is not for me, it seems, to touch the sky with my two arms,"[32] we yearn to do what we cannot. And we see acts of bringing in our own imagined worlds as we read: "Evening Star, you bring back all that was scattered in the shimmer of Dawn. You bring the sheep, you bring the goat, and you bring her child to the mother."[33] So close are these lines to life that one must be truly alive in reading them:

For as I look at you, if only for an instant,
my voice no longer comes to me.
My silent tongue is broken,
and a quick and subtle flame
runs up beneath my skin.
I lose my sense of sight, hear only drumming in my ears.
I drip cold sweat,
and a trembling chases all through me.
I am greener than the pale grass
and it seems to me that I am close to death.[34]

In the following poem, we are so captured by the images in these lines,

> There are those who say
> an array of horsemen,
> and others of marching men,
> and others of ships, is
> the most beautiful thing on the dark earth,[35]

that we are startled by what follows: "But I say it is whatever one loves."[36]

It is trite to say that lines such as these move us; it is closer to the sense of them to say that they move and we are carried along with them. In speaking of the Muses, Sappho writes, "By teaching me their art they honored me."[37] Art like Sappho's teaches us, the readers, that our lives will be artful insofar as we yearn to exist as do those whom the poet portrays. It is not so much the poetry as art, but the kind of living we might have enjoyed, that is "the rose of the Muses" in these lines:

> When you have died, there will be nothing.
> No memory of you will remain,
> not a trace
> to linger after:
> you do not share
> the rose of the Muses with us,
> and will wander unseen
> in the hall of the dead,
> a fitful shade among the blinded ghosts.[38]

Not to leave any art in one's name is to be unknown to posterity. Yet surely Sappho, along with Homer and Pindar, thinks that one's deeds, real, imagined, hoped-for, are what art memorializes. The finest rose of our muses is a life lived, consisting of deeds rather than words.

Sappho expresses a purity of life so intimate in its detachment from the affairs of the polis that it may be what Plato had in mind when he wrote of "virtue-in-itself," of "forms, eternal and changeless." Yet Sappho's virtues are full of life, charged with action, never adequately settled in the nature of things to satisfy the requirements of a Platonic form. Sappho's purity is not that of Polyxena, a purity of innocence. Sappho's is worldly-wise, despite its detachment from political matters. While not written to extol "public"virtues, the way in which Sappho's lyrics share with the reader the need for integrity of being makes them intimate and personal examples of Greek art. As a particular sculpture makes public an ideal, Sappho's poems make public an ideal grounded in the reality of human beings striving to say what they are, and wanting to share that way of being with others.

In tragic poetry and in Sappho's lyrics we see that conduct is inescapably social, yet we have not made explicit the social dimension of human nature, which was to have such a prominent place in Aristotle. In his work, the disposition to form relationships with others is as natural as the disposition to seek ends of certain kinds. Indeed, if we are to conduct ourselves as human beings, we have to do so through relationships with others. Of course a kind of relationship exists among Homer's noble heroes and in Pindar's band of heroic champions, among the poets who extol heroic deeds and the philosophers who try to understand all this. Natural nobility is shared by the fortunate few who need a social context in which to share their blessings, their achievements, their hopes. We may think of them as if their common natures need Aristotle's conception of the poliscraft to most fully actualize themselves. Pericles puts it well, in speaking of Athens: "Here each individual is interested not only in his own affairs but in the affairs of the state as well . . . we do not say that a man who takes no interest in politics is a man who minds his own business; we say that he has no business here at all."[39]

In Isocrates' characterization of oratory as "the good man speaking well," we find the social nature of human beings so much a part of his work that it is at least second nature, if it is not indeed first nature. The social nature of human beings is present in Isocrates' writings in four ways: (1) In his aim that the work of the orator stand alongside the work of the poet in its cultural and educational significance; (2) In his portrayal of noble birth and exceptional virtue in the ancient Athenians, and the ideal which that nature holds forth for Athenians of his day; (3) In his conception of the requisites for undertaking an education in oratory; and (4) In his idea that a certain kind of culture sets Greeks apart from barbarians. In discussing each of these, we shall see that it is conduct of a certain kind which Isocrates wants to bring into being. The orator is to celebrate it, even as poets do; the young are to be trained to act in certain ways before they are capable of understanding why they acted as they did. Finally, the kind of culture which he espouses is itself an ideal of conduct, of living a life with others.

First, Isocrates compares his work with that of Pindar in its glorification of Athens as the "bulwark of Hellas."[40] The possible significance of oratory as an expression of the meaning of one's life is set forth by Isocrates in *Antidosis,* in which he defends his own life and character:

> I came ... to the ... conclusion ... that the only way in which I could accomplish this was to compose a discourse which would be, as it were, a true image of my thought and of my whole life; for I hope that this would serve both as the best means of making known the truth about me and, at the same time, as a monument, after my death, more noble than statues of bronze.[41]

Further, in Isocrates' repeated references to the Athenians' noble ancestors, we are reminded of Pindar's praises of valorous activity by the nobly born. When his contemporaries' actions fall short of the promise in their noble ancestry, Isocrates takes them to task:

> I reproach men in private life when they succeed in a few things and fail in many, and regard them as falling short of what they ought to be; and, more than that, when men are sprung from noble ancestors and yet are only a little better than those who are distinguished for depravity, and much worse than their fathers, I rebuke them and would counsel them to cease from being what they are. And I am of the same mind also regarding public affairs.[42]

Thus the first way of characterizing the social nature of human beings joins with and merges into the second. Poetry and oratory celebrate the place of noble birth in human conduct and, by the examples of nobility so portrayed, urge on the listeners to strive to actualize the ideal of nobility in their own conduct. Next, the requisites for undertaking training in oratory are just what one would expect who has read Pindar's adulation of the nobly born, and who has witnessed Isocrates' fascination with those so born: (a) students must have natural aptitude; (b) they must train and master the subject matters needed in their craft; and (c) they must practice their craft.[43] In saying that students must do these things "if they are to excel in oratory or in managing affairs or in any line of work,"[44] Isocrates repeats the wisdom in Phoenix' aim for Achilles, to make him a speaker *and* a man of action. Not only is action the end of education, but it is a certain quality of action that enables one to excel. The aim is for the good orator to become the best.

The insistence on excelling, on acting according to the best of which human beings are capable, is manifested in the causes which the orator addresses: speeches and discourses should be in support of "great and honorable" causes. What is more, the social responsibility is apparent in Isocrates' claim that the causes worth supporting are "devoted to the welfare of men and our common good," rather than to petty or private interests. Despite the differences of context, the similarities with Pindar are apparent in Isocrates' claim that the speaker or writer of worth "will select from all the actions of men which bear upon his subject those examples which are the most illustrious and the most edifying"; Isocrates continues, one who has the habit of using such examples "will feel their influence not only in the preparation of a given discourse but in all the actions of his life."[45] The ultimate end is by now apparent: natural aptitude, study, and practice are for the sake of action which strives to be conduct of the highest kind.

When we turn to Plato, again we find an appeal for a certain kind of conduct. It is an appeal for an end never realized yet sought by an activity of the highest kind—philosophic activity. Of all the ancient philosophers Plato is the one most renowned for stating an ideal that is beyond ordinary activity. He is at his best in his characterizations of the activity of seeking an ideal, rather than in assuring us that the ideal sought either had been actualized or is capable of being actualized. The effort to gain the ideal is frustrated every time because the very nature of the end that is sought forbids even extraordinary human activity from realizing it. Such an end remains beyond the reach of human beings, accessible only to godlike beings.

In Plato's early dialogues, Socrates seeks a meaning of certain virtues, such as courage, friendship, and beauty, about which the participants can reach agreement. Each dialogue ends as Socrates finds that people do not know what they originally thought they knew; that every opinion as to the nature of a virtue can be countered by a different opinion. As Socrates' investigations proceed, he moves away from seeking the meaning of the separate virtues and asks, instead, what is "virtue-in-itself". In the *Meno*, he presses the point that it is one virtue that needs to be known, not many:

> What is that character in respect of which they don't differ at all, but are all the same? . . . While the nature of virtue as a whole [virtue-in-itself] is still under question, don't suppose that you can explain it to anyone in terms of its parts, or by any similar type of explanation. Understand rather that the same question needs to be answered; you say this and that about virtue, but what *is* it?[46]

Admitting that he does not know what virtue is "in itself," Socrates says to Meno, "Nevertheless I am ready to carry out, together with you, a joint investigation and inquiry into what it is."[47] "Virtue-in-itself" is both the aim of the investigation and that which makes the investigation worth doing. It is what we are looking for, and the standard involved in the looking. The close connection between virtue as a kind of knowledge and virtue as an activity of body and soul is suggested in this passage:

> The soul, since it is immortal and has been born many times, and has seen all things both here and in the other world, has learned everything that is. So we need not be surprised if it can recall the knowledge of virtue or anything else which, as we see, it once possessed. All nature is akin, and the soul has learned everything, so that when a man has recalled a single piece of knowledge—*learned* it, in ordinary language—there is no reason why he should not find out all the rest, if he keeps a stout heart and does not grow weary of the search; for seeking and learning are in fact nothing but recollection.[48]

Two emphases in this passage join Plato to the poets who preceded him and to Aristotle who followed him. First, the use of the myth on the immortality of the soul to make a point. And, second, the need for activity of seeking and learning. To put them together: the truth that is contained in the myth can only be *known* by human activity. Of course, Socrates' myth and its moral do not enable us to understand the nature of virtue. While it does not show us what virtue is, it tells us that we must engage ourselves in an active way in searching. Virtue-in-itself will come, if at all, by an activity that is akin to recollecting: this is not merely a mental affair, but a combined activity of mind and body. There is a kind of paradox in the conclusion Socrates reaches at the end of the *Meno*: "On our present reasoning, then, whoever has virtue gets it by divine dispensation. But we shall not understand the truth of the matter until, before asking how men get virtue, we try to discover what virtue is in and by itself."[49] Plato appears to be suggesting that discovering what virtue is is something that we should try first; and *then* we may ask how we get virtue. Yet this is only appearance; in actuality Plato shows us that it is in the activity of discovering virtue that we find out how to get virtue. This is to say that *knowing* virtue will happen only if we *get* virtue. The evidence for this interpretation lies in Plato's dialogues if they are read as dramatic accounts of activity in search of virtue. The very activity of the participants is the action which leads to discovery (insofar as anything is discovered); and the test of whether virtue has been discovered lies in the activities of the discoverers. Again: the only way to *get* virtue is to discover it; and only if it is discovered have we *got* it.

The dialogue as a "joint investigation and inquiry into what [virtue] is" is Plato's philosophic counterpart of Pindar's "drive to gigantic glory". The philosopher in quest of virtue-in-itself strives to gain "joy of victory." For the philosopher the victory is over ignorance, over sophistry in its various forms, and over one's own limitations. And by saying that "whoever has virtue gets it by divine dispensation," Plato is repeating the ancient wisdom celebrated by Pindar, that only those favored by nature's gods are capable of the great deed. Here he joins with Pindar and with Isocrates in his insistence that nature's gift is necessary, but not sufficient, to gain virtue. At times, the prospects for human activity alone appear to be dim indeed. At one place in the *Laws*, for example, Plato calls human beings puppets of the gods;[50] again, he says that human beings may be likened to puppets, "for the most part."[51] Clearly this is a recognition of human limitations. It is as if the striving by which we investigate the nature of virtue-in-itself is the way of finding out what our limits are; again we cannot *know* what they are except through the activity by which we find our limits.

The philosophic activity of striving to know our limits puts us in mind of Aristotle's later discussion of matters of conduct in the *Nicomachean Ethics*: "In doing the end cannot be other than itself; doing well is in itself the end."[52] What we find in Plato's dialogues is not virtue-in-itself, but human beings striving mightily and, in the quality of conduct that *is* the striving, is to be found whatever virtue they gain. Insofar as they "do well," i.e., insofar as they gain an element of understanding at the end of the dialogue which they did not have at the beginning, we would say, along with Aristotle, *that* is the end. Plato resists an idea like Aristotle's, "that matters of fact admit of variation,"[53] if this means that they *must* be variable. Surely he agrees with Aristotle that, in fact, most human conduct is variable. What Plato seeks, in virtue-in-itself, is an object of knowledge that is also the cause of knowledge. In the *Republic*, Plato calls such an object the "Form of the Good," or "Goodness," and says that it is "beyond truth and knowledge":

> This, then, which gives to the objects of knowledge their truth and to him who knows them his power of knowing, is the Form or essential nature of Goodness. It is the cause of knowledge and truth; and so, while you may think of it as an object of knowledge, you will do well to regard it as something beyond truth and knowledge and, precious as these both are, of still higher worth.[54]

Yet at the end of Plato's dialogues, we do not know "virtue-in-itself" or "Goodness," and none of the investigators in the dialogues knows these objects. At most, we must join with Aristotle and say that the investigators have "done well"; or, to paraphrase Pindar, "They have sought out some measure in things gained"; or we may be grateful, along with Isocrates, that one who has the habit of using such examples as the philosophic participants in Plato's dialogues "will feel their influence . . . in all the actions of his life."

In his own way, Plato emphasizes human limitations, while insisting on the kind of striving which tries to understand what the limitations are, even while aiming to overcome them by trying to know virtue-in-itself. In saying that human beings may be likened to playthings of the gods, "for the most part," he is pointing to our limitations; at the same time, we shall not understand what they are unless we strive not merely to understand, but to overcome them.

The story of human striving, working to its fullest yet unable to gain "the veritable knowledge of Being that veritably is,"[55] which only the gods may know, is told in the *Phaedrus*, where the human soul is characterized as two winged horses drawing a chariot with a winged driver. As for human souls, they cannot live the life of gods; of the best of them, who remind us of Pindar's precious few, and of Isocrates' orators, Plato says:

> Of the other souls that which best follows a god and becomes most like thereunto raises her Charioteer's head into the outer region, and is carried round with the gods in the revolution, but being confounded by her Steeds she has much ado to discern the things that are; another now rises, and now sinks, and by reason of her unruly steeds sees in part, but in part sees not. As for the rest, though all are eager to reach the heights and seek to follow, they are not able: sucked down as they travel they trample and tread upon one another, this one striving to outstrip that. Thus confusion ensues, and conflict and grievous sweat: whereupon, with their charioteers powerless, many are lamed, and many have their wings all broken; and for all their toiling they are baulked, every one, of the full vision of Being, and departing therefrom, they feed upon the food of semblance.[56]

According to this story, Plato's best souls only gain an understanding that falls short of virtue-in-itself, and hence are doomed by their own activity to know semblance, not true Being. Yet what stands out here is the passion for striving, for taking action, even though human souls, at best, can only "follow gods." Limited as Aristotle's poliscraftsmen will be, Plato's charioteers "see" in part, and in part "see not." Our activities, while enabling us to see some things, get in the way of seeing other things, and become part of the problem that we are trying to solve. We are forced, once again, to make do with the idea that the quality of human life lies in action itself; or one might say that the quality of human life *is* the action. What we see happening in Plato's dialogues is the act itself as the only end that human beings realize. In characterizing human conduct with its limitations made clear, the agony of the action is emphasized in Plato's account of conduct, expressed as a passion to go where the gods go, but having to settle for merely human ways of being and of knowing.

Chapter 3

ARISTOTLE'S POLISCRAFT

Aristotle's work is an analysis of the ways in which human beings take action as a part of their nature. It is a declaration of the idea that we cannot avoid making our own social and political nature. Since to be social is to be human, we make our own human nature. Aristotle's naturalism stands out in the idea that things of nature have ends. Human beings are things of nature, no less than fishes are. For Aristotle this means that human activities of knowing, doing, and making have ends which are natural in their own way. While his naturalism extends into all activities in which human beings engage, human beings are not superior to other natural things according to some inherent purpose in nature. This is to say that natural processes are not designed *for* human beings. Yet human beings, and human beings alone, are capable of understanding the world in which they find themselves, of doing worthwhile things, and of making worthwhile things. Although the world was not created for human beings, it is for them to understand, if they become disposed to try. Yet they were not made to understand it; they have to learn how to do so; and what they know, make, and do is their responsibility. What they must choose to know, to do, and to make is not written in the nature of things; it must be found out in the knowing, the doing, the making. Here we are interested, primarily, in Aristotle's conception of doing, in which his ideas about conduct are worked out. At the same time, his ideas on conduct are understood in relation to knowing and making, as Aristotle's contextualism demands.

Aristotle's discussions of conduct are worked out most fully in his *Nicomachean Ethics* and *Politics*, what Max Fisch calls his poliscraft.[1] The "ultimate end," Aristotle says, which is the "Supreme Good," the one "we wish for its own sake, while we wish the others only for the sake of this,"[2] is the object of a "master craft." Understanding the master craft is the aim of the science of politics.[3] "The end of this science," Aristotle goes on, "must include the ends of all the others. Therefore, the Good of man must be the end of the science of Politics."[4]

Thus the object of the *Nicomachean Ethics*, the good of men, cannot be realized unless the *Politics* also is considered. The two works taken together constitute the poliscraft, which investigates matters such as the branches of study citizens are to undertake. It employs the rest of the sciences in determining which actions to take, and "lays down laws as to what people shall do and what things they shall refrain from doing."[5]

In what sense is the poliscraft a *craft*, and in what sense is it a *science*? Aristotle treats this matter in two ways. First, near the beginning of *Nicomachean Ethics,* he explains what sort of subjects are investigated in the science of politics in a general way. Second, he works out in detail the nature of the virtues by which human beings conduct themselves in both the *Nicomachean Ethics* and *Politics.* In doing so, he shows by illustration what sort of investigation he claims the science of politics to be. At the same time his characterizations of the virtues make up the subject matter by which we come to understand that the poliscraft has a practical nature. This nature is made in doing, in learning how to conduct ourselves.

The science of politics is different from the theoretical sciences, whose nature is to know; and from the arts, whose nature is to make. As we move from Aristotle's introducing the nature of the science of politics to his considering the nature of the virtues and the sort of community in which it may be possible to actualize the virtues, we learn that *knowing* the nature of the science of politics is not to bring the virtues into being. We learn that knowing the science of politics is not sufficient to realize the end of the poliscraft. This is because the *craft* of the polis involves doing, acting in certain ways to bring into existence the Supreme Good recognized by the science in a polis of a certain kind. Inasmuch as acting is a necessary condition for realizing the nature of the poliscraft, there is a sense in which we can know its nature in the fullest possible way by striving to bring into existence a polis of a certain kind.

Now we turn to Aristotle's characterization of the nature of the investigation of the master craft. After pointing out that the subjects studied there, such as "moral nobility and justice," involve opinions and uncertainty, he writes:

> We must therefore be content if, in dealing with subjects and starting from premises thus uncertain, we succeed in presenting a broad outline of the truth; when our subjects and our premises are merely generalities, it is enough if we arrive at generally valid conclusions. Accordingly we may ask the student also to accept the various views we put forward in the same spirit; for it is the mark of an educated mind to expect that amount of exactness in each kind which the nature of the particular subject admits. It is equally unreasonable to accept merely probable conclusions from a mathematician and to demand strict demonstration from an orator.[6]

He goes on to say that it is the "experience of life and conduct . . . that supply the premises and subject matter"[7] of the master craft. In discussing the Supreme Good which is the end of the poliscraft, Aristotle points out that there exist many goods, recognizing that "good appears to be one thing in one pursuit or art and another in another: it is different in medicine from what it is in strategy, and so on."[8] Aristotle asks, "What definition of the Good then will hold true in all the arts? Perhaps we may define it as that for the sake of which everything else is done."[9] Remember that he had characterized the Supreme Good as the one we wish for its own sake, and the others only for its sake. Now that which is "chosen always as an end and never as a means" is happiness.[10]

Aristotle observes that the goodness of a craftsman who has some function to perform "is thought to reside in that function."[11] In seeking the nature of the function of man, Aristotle supposes that:

> If we declare that the function of man is a certain form of life, and define that form of life as the exercise of the soul's faculties and activities in association with rational principle, and say that the function of a good man is to perform these activities well and rightly, and if a function is well performed when it is performed in accordance with its own proper excellence—from these premises it follows that the Good of man is the active exercise of his soul's faculties in conformity with excellence or virtue, or if there be several human excellences or virtues, in conformity with the best and most perfect among them. Moreover this activity must occupy a complete lifetime; for one swallow does not make spring, nor does one fine day; and similarly one day or a brief period of happiness does not make a man supremely blessed and happy.[12]

Aristotle calls this account a rough sketch, a beginning, and points to the necessity of filling it in afterwards. In other words, what it means to "perform a function in accord with its own excellence," " to exercise the soul's faculties in association with rational principle," and so on, must be accounted for in the particular lines of inquiry that the investigators are capable of working out. Later in the *Nicomachean Ethics,* Aristotle qualifies his characterization of the "Good of man" as "the active exercise of the soul's faculties in conformity with excellence or virtue" by saying, "Virtue is not merely a disposition conforming to right principle, but one cooperating with right principle."[13] This adds a new dimension to action. It emphasizes the deliberative element in action by holding forth the possibility that virtuous action can be deliberately principled; the mere conformity of disposition to principle suggests a nondeliberative relationship in conduct. Aristotle seeks something more: in the possibility that virtue may be deliberately principled is the prospect that human beings may make a difference in their conduct rather than merely conform to principles of conduct already laid down.

Another kind of beginning needs to be mentioned here, inasmuch as it reveals Aristotle's confidence that the prevailing conventional wisdom stands for something about which we can have a reasonable degree of confidence. "It is proper to start from the known," he says, and adds that "the known" has two meanings—"what is known to us," and "what is knowable in itself."[14] He then says that it is proper to begin with "what is known to us," adding that, if it is satisfactorily ascertained that "the starting point or first principle is the fact that a thing is so," then "there is no need also to know the reason why it is so."[15] This is repeated later, when Aristotle has established his rough sketch of the conception of happiness that is the end sought by the Poliscraft. At the beginning of the Poliscraft, Aristotle maintains, we cannot expect to begin with something that is "knowable in itself," one kind of first principle; we must be content to begin with another kind of first principle, the conception of happiness which is "known to us." The "fact that this principle is so" *is* the "primary thing," the first principle that has been established.[16] It must be examined "not only as a logical conclusion deduced from certain premises but also in the light of the current opinions on the subject."[17]

Aristotle's discussion of "beginnings" and "first principles" is another illustration of his idea that the nature of the beginning is part of the nature of the subject matter itself ("the beginning is admittedly more than half of the whole")[18]. It must take its shape from the nature of the subject under investigation. At the same time, it shapes the subject. The nature of the Poliscraft simply does not enable us to begin our investigation with "what is knowable in itself." If we could do this, no investigation would be necessary. At the beginning, our *possible* actions are in question; at the same time we must begin with what is already "known to us," which is a result of the past actions that gave shape to the conventional wisdom in whose midst we examine logical conclusions deduced from premises. In recalling Aristotle's claim that the premises and subject matter of the poliscraft are found in the "experience of life and conduct," we get a sense of the significance of poetry, oratory, history, and philosophical writings for Aristotle's search for beginnings. It is to human experience in its various forms that we must look, Aristotle is saying to us, if we are to find our beginnings. This is why Aristotle takes so seriously the writings of his predecessors: While it is true that "what is known to them" is not "what is knowable in itself," it must be understood that we are subject to limitations, even as they were. We may know different things from them, and thereby have progressed in our understanding, yet we share with them the necessity of beginning our investigations of the poliscraft as an experience of life and conduct with what is known to us rather than with what is knowable in itself.

What Aristotle wants us to understand is that logical conclusions reached as first principles of the Poliscraft are not only *about* action, but are derived from opinions formulated in the midst of actions whose participants are uncertain about the outcomes of the craft in which they are engaged. They are shaped in the midst of action, and as they take shape and grow, they constitute a different action foreseen, which means that a different experience is made possible for those engaged in the poliscraft. The logic involved is not just about action but is a *kind* of action.

In turning to Aristotle's characterization of the nature and production of the virtues, we see the importance laid to the notion of an investigation that requires a way of conduct which is at once the means and the end of the investigation itself. Virtue is of two kinds, moral and intellectual. The moral virtues are produced by habit, the intellectual virtues by instruction.[19] First, we shall discuss the moral virtues. "The [moral] virtues," Aristotle writes, "are engendered in us neither by nature nor yet in violation of nature; nature gives us the capacity to receive them, and this capacity is brought to maturity by habit."[20] Thus we are not naturally brave or temperate; by nature we have the capacity to become brave and temperate. Put in another way: "The faculties given us by nature are bestowed on us first in a potential form; we exhibit their actual exercise afterwards."[21] It is by taking action of certain kinds that we learn to actualize our potential virtues. We acquire the virtues by practicing them: "We become just by doing just acts, temperate by doing temperate acts, brave by doing brave acts."[22] This is not a mere truism for Aristotle, because he wants to emphasize the differences among qualities of acts; e.g., human beings will be produced by certain kinds of acts, but the point is to produce the best of the kind whether the kind in question be brave, temperate, or just.

The emphasis on habit in training young children in moral virtues lies in the inability of the very young to control their conduct by principle. "Children cannot be happy," Aristotle writes, "for they are not old enough to be capable of noble acts; when children are spoken of as happy it is in compliment to their promise for the future."[23] In recalling the requirements for actualizing the Supreme Good, we remember that happiness requires not only that one actively exercise one's soul in cooperation with the highest virtue, but that one needs a complete lifetime to do this. Stated in terms of moral and intellectual virtues, the aim is for children first to learn the moral virtues by habit; and later, as their intellectual virtues are being educated, they conduct themselves according to the principles of intellect. Put differently, they will be able to conduct themselves in the moral virtues learned by habit and in the intellectual virtues learned through instruction: Only then are they capable of becoming happy, i.e., of conducting themselves in cooperation with the highest principles of their moral and intellectual nature.

In turning to Aristotle's more precise definition of moral virtue, we learn two things. First, moral virtue is exercised when one hits the mean between two extremes, e.g., Courage is the mean between fear and confidence, Greatness of Soul is the mean between smallness of soul and vanity. It is easy to miss, and difficult to hit the exact mark, Aristotle points out, quoting a verse whose wisdom tells us, "Goodness is simple, badness manifold."[24] Second, we see the connection between the moral virtues and the intellectual virtues. At the same time, Aristotle thinks that there is a sense in which intellect is capable of determining action. Aristotle defines moral virtue as:

> a settled disposition of the mind determining the choice of actions and emotions, consisting essentially in the observance of the mean and relative to us, this being determined by principle, that is, as the prduent man would determine it.[25]

Both the moral virtues and the intellectual virtue, prudence, are kinds of action, as Aristotle has been leading us to see all along. His definition of moral virtue here is another way of telling us that the poliscraft is not merely a rational investigation, but one with a practical aim. At one point he goes so far as to say:

> (We are not investigating the nature of virtue for the sake of knowing what it is, but in order that we may become good, without which result our investigation would be of no use), we have consequently to carry our enquiry into the region of conduct, and to ask how we are to act rightly.[26]

This recalls the idea discussed earlier that the end of the poliscraft is to bring a polis of a certain kind into being, not merely to know the science of politics.

The aim of the poliscraft, then, is not merely "intellectual," but "practical" as well; or, if one presses the point, the practical aim is uppermost. Here Aristotle shows himself to be heir to the tradition of Plato, despite Aristotle's alleged differences from it. For Aristotle, the aim of the investigation is to become good, rather than to know what virtue is. Here we find an affinity with Plato's idea that "knowledge is virtue." In a fundamental way, Aristotle is not denying Plato's claim. Aristotle's idea, that we begin with what is known to us in order to suggest certain kinds of conduct that conform to the Supreme Good is joined with another idea, that "what is known to us" is a necessary condition for gaining the highest virtue. If the necessary condition is to help us realize the Supreme Good, then we must recognize that "what is known to us" is a beginning, not an end. In any case, as "known," the beginning "calls for," or requires a certain conduct which is needed in order to "actualize" virtue, to turn what is practicable into what is practical. Thus for Aristotle, no less than for Plato, knowing what virtue is is a kind of conduct. Indeed, in its highest form, it would be the supreme union of knowledge and virtue which shows us that virtue is not *applied* knowledge, but is a *kind* of knowledge. It is knowledge in the sense that it is an idea joined with the conduct that spells out the meaning of the idea; and it is virtue in the sense that virtue is a way of being in the world that gives expression to the highest kind of knowledge that human beings are capable of realizing. To say it in another way: Virtue *is* the highest knowledge that we are capable of realizing.

Thus, in the poliscraft, acting in certain ways is the very conduct that is required by the knowledge with which the investigation begins; and, ultimately, the beginning knowledge leads to further knowledge and further conduct. In this sense, to know is to do, and to know better is to do better. To understand more fully the sense in which knowing *requires* a kind of conduct and, at the same time, *is* a kind of conduct, we may turn to Aristotle's discussion of the intellectual virtues. Here we come to terms again with Aristotle's idea that we investigate the nature of virtue for the sake of becoming good rather than for the sake of knowing what virtue is.

Aristotle begins his discussion of the intellectual virtues by assuming that there are five qualities of the soul through which the mind receives truth. They are called "art, scientific knowledge, prudence, wisdom, and intelligence."[27] Here we are concerned with scientific knowledge, art, and prudence. Objects of scientific knowledge, he says, exist of necessity.[28] He goes on to say that scientific knowledge is the quality of soul "whereby we demonstrate."[29] That is to say, we "demonstrate" when we know that the first principles are more certain than the conclusions drawn from them.

Aristotle goes on to write of a class of things different from those known by scientific knowledge. It is a "class of things that admit of variation" which "includes both things made and actions done."[30] The rational quality of soul concerned with doing, he says, is different from that concerned with making. Art, one of the qualities of soul that is concerned with variable things, brings things into existence; the efficient cause lies in the maker, not in the thing made; at the same time, he says, art is not concerned with doing.[31] The other quality of soul, prudence, that belongs to the class of variable things, differs from art in that art, or making, "aims at an end distinct from the act of making, whereas in doing the end cannot be other than the act itself; doing well is in itself the end."[32]

Aristotle's discussion of the poliscraft arrives at its most critical point with this idea. Now we can understand why Aristotle insisted on the idea that it is necessary to begin the investigation in the midst of probability rather than certainty. We understand also why the nature of the subject matter involves experience of life and conduct, which we cannot expect to know in the sense in which we can know the objects of scientific knowledge, which exist by necessity. If, in prudence, "doing well is in itself the end," and if prudence is the essential virtue sought by the poliscraft, we see clearly why the poliscraft, as investigated in the *Nicomachean Ethics* and the *Politics,* is a continuing activity, not one to be terminated by reaching a demonstrated conclusion derived from first principles. "To be a matter of scientific knowledge," Aristotle writes, "a truth must be demonstrated by deduction from other truths; while art and prudence are concerned only with things that admit of variation."[33] The lesson is made clear: in affairs of prudence, the soul deals with variable things. It is apparent also that Aristotle believes that such things cannot have their natures shaped so that they will conform to the objects of scientific knowledge. This is to say that affairs of prudence do not yield truth in the sense that truth is capable of being gained as scientific knowledge. To say that the subject matter of the poliscraft "admits of variation" is to say that it does not yield "scientific" truth. In admitting that the subject matter of the poliscraft is variable, Aristotle characterizes the prudent man in a way that reminds us of Isocrates' description of an educated man as one who generally arrives at the right course of action. Instead of aiming for scientific knowledge in the poliscraft, "it is held to be the mark of a prudent man to be able to deliberate well about what is good and advantageous for himself, not in some one department . . . but what is advantageous as a means to the good life in general . . . the prudent man in general will be the man who is good at deliberating in general."[34] It is just because "one cannot deliberate about things that are of necessity,"[35] that the subject matters of scientific knowledge are not those of the prudent man, and the matters to which the prudent man subjects himself cannot be treated in ways that yield "scientific truth."

If we return to Aristotle's maxim that the investigation of the poliscraft must begin with what is "known to us" rather than with what is "knowable in itself," we now see that the poliscraft can only continue and end with what is known to us; in the poliscraft we cannot expect to grasp what is knowable in itself. By the nature of the subject matter, we are forced to deal with different versions of what is known to us; what these versions have in common is their variability; they differ in their different ways of doing. Yet inasmuch as doing (in certain ways) is the means, while doing (in certain other ways that are "happier") is the end, what we cannot expect to capture is an end distinct from the doing. Through doing, as both means and ends, we strive to alter the quality of life and conduct for the better, to live in happiness in the best state which our natures are capable of bringing into existence.

Now we understand a sense in which the nature of prudence, by which we conduct ourselves with the aim of becoming happy by acting in cooperation with the highest virtue, is itself an activity. Its nature is determined by activity: the quality of earlier activity affects later activity. In learning to do certain things well, e.g., exercise the moral virtues, we become moral and prepare ourselves to become intellectual as well. In particular, we learn the intellectual virtue prudence. This means that prudence is a virtue in process of development. Inasmuch as we can only develop our *human* nature in a community of human beings, the nature of the community needs to be investigated. Indeed, it is necessary to bring the right kind of community into being if prudence is to be actualized to its fullest. That is why the science of politics includes both the *Nicomachean Ethics* and the *Politics*. "The best method of investigation," Aristotle says in the *Politics*, "is to study things in the process of development from the beginning."[36] Starting with the "first coupling together of persons," we find that the development of the first partnership leads to the household, the partnership of households leads to the village, and out of the partnership of villages comes the polis.[37] With the polis the partnership "has at last attained the limit of virtually complete self-sufficiency, and thus, while it comes into existence for the sake of life, it exists for the good life."[38]

Thus the social dimension of human nature that is required as the context in which prudence can be actualized most fully is now made explicit. Since we actualize our moral and intellectual virtues only insofar as we learn to do virtuous acts, so we actualize our political nature by understanding the end for which the first partnership, and then the next exists. We thus continue until we understand the ultimate end for which all partnerships exist. Because we can come to actualize our moral and intellectual natures most fully only in a certain kind of partnership, a city-state, we can come to actualize our political nature most fully only as we act in certain ways, as we exercise our moral and intellectual virtues. "Every city-state exists by nature, inasmuch as the first partnerships so exist," Aristotle writes, "for the city-state is the end of the other partnerships, and nature is an end, since that which each thing is when its growth is completed we speak of as being the nature of each thing."[39] Yet it is clear that, even if we accept the political nature of human beings which Aristotle considers, the *quality* of each partnership is not given, but must be developed through human activity. When he says that "the city-state is a natural growth, and that man is by nature a political animal,"[40] Aristotle does not suggest that the exact quality of activity is given. What is given are certain limits in whose contexts human beings strive to become happy in the best states. Remember that the Poliscraft is a "craft," not the kind of science whose truths can be deduced by necessity from other truths. In striving to become happy in the best polis, we must learn to be content with probabilities. In short, we must strive to exercise prudence, rather than try to gain scientific knowledge.

As "doing well is in itself the end" of doing, then we may say that doing well is our moral and intellectual nature: it is "that which each thing is when its growth is completed." At the same time, if we follow Aristotle's advice and "study things in the process of development from the beginning," we must be sensitive to a kind of nature different from its nature when its growth is completed. This is an incomplete nature, in fact a process involving many incomplete natures which things have in the process of their development. We may say that things have an ultimate nature, and several proximate natures. In one sense, the ultimate nature which we investigators have in mind directs our investigations from the beginning; it puts us in mind of processes and hence of proximate natures which are incomplete in comparison with the ultimate nature they are capable of becoming; yet they have natures in themselves. For example, a village is not the ultimate partnership, the polis, which is the end of our political activity; yet a village has a nature in itself with its own ends. While we may lead the good life of most nearly complete happiness in a city-state, we may lead a life of incomplete happiness in a village.

We may take the nature of children as another example of a process of development. The child is said to possess the deliberative part of the soul, "but in an undeveloped form,"[41] Aristotle writes. To say that the child is potentially an adult is to say that a child can only become an adult by first learning moral virtues as a condition of deliberating. When the developing person can deliberate, e.g., can choose among possible means for securing the highest ends, he will be exercising prudence. Yet in the process of becoming an adult the child takes on several natures, each of which is incomplete if compared with the nature of prudence in its completeness. "The child is not completely developed," Aristotle continues, "so that manifestly his virtue also is not personal to himself, but relative to the fully developed being, that is, the person in authority over him."[42] It should be noted that there are two senses in which the "fully developed being" may be said to be in authority over the child. One sense is that in which a particular teacher is in authority over a particular child; another sense is that in which the fully developed being is *present* in the actual child, i.e., a nondeliberative child has the potentiality of becoming a deliberative adult. To put it another way, a child lacking prudence has the potentiality of becoming prudent. These two senses are recognized in this statement: "The appetitive part of us should be ruled by principle, just as a boy should live in obedience to his tutor."[43]

The nature of things which Aristotle has in mind does not determine the specific qualities of conduct, whether conduct be considered from the perspective of the various partnerships in the development of the polis, or from the perspective of the various proximate natures which human beings take on in the course of their development toward becoming complete human beings. The nature of things done in the poliscraft may be thought of as general limits which we cannot exceed, and as the aim of the conduct itself as we act in certain ways. As the ultimate end of conduct, a certain nature is that *at* which we aim. And as the starting point of the investigation, it is that *by* which we take aim. Aristotle has told us that we begin our investigations with what is known to us; in the Poliscraft, we begin with the aim of becoming happy in the best state. In the beginning, the aim is a potentiality; happiness in the best state is not yet actualized. To say that it is in our nature to become actualized in a certain way is not to promise that we will in fact be actualized in any particular way. (That is why Aristotle tells us that as one swallow does not make spring, so one happy day does not make a happy person.)

The act of reason by which we begin with an aim, e.g., the recognition of the end of the poliscraft, has its counterpart in his treatise *On the Parts of Animals*. There he likens works of art to works of nature, saying that "reason forms the starting point, alike in the works of art and in works of nature,"[44] and that the starting point is "that which is to be."[45] The counterpart in the *Nicomachean Ethics* and the *Politics* is beginning with the idea that "happiness is to be." We aim to act in ways so that we strive to bring happiness into being in the best polis that we can develop. In the *Eudemian Ethics*, Aristotle puts the relationship between thought and action in this way: "The End is the starting point of the process of thought, but the conclusion of the process of thought is the starting point of action."[46] Again, the action by which reason forms the starting point is a kind of conduct while the actions by which we move from the starting point to the end of our investigation are conduct also. If we gain happiness, it will be a kind of conduct, not something apart from conduct.

It is proper to conclude the discussion of Aristotle's conception of the poliscraft by making explicit the sense in which his theory of conduct is a theory of education. In the most general sense, of course, learning to take action in ways that aim to bring about happiness in the best state is an undertaking of education, insofar as education is a process by which mind and character take shape. In this general sense, learning the moral and intellectual virtues is an enterprise whose nature is social in an inescapable way. It is natural for human beings to be ethical and social, but the particular kind of ethical and social beings that we become is an empirical matter. At one point, Aristotle puts it in this way: "It is proper to follow the division of nature, for all art and education aim at filling up nature's deficiencies."[47] "Nature's deficiencies" require particular ways for us to act in order to provide the context in which art and education do their work. The nature which human beings ultimately "ought to possess" is happiness.[48]

Thus nonhuman "nature" is not alone in having deficiencies; human beings are part of nature and capable of conduct that is deficient in its own ways. Human deficiencies are part of nature's deficiencies. What human beings ought to do, and what they do in fact, may be far apart: "Between reason and habit the most perfect harmony ought to exist," Aristotle writes, "as it is possible both for the reason to have missed the highest principle and for men to have been as wrongly trained through habits."[49] Thus it is as essential for our original nature, i.e., our nature as children, as it is for our ultimate nature, i.e., our highest possible nature as happy people living in the best polis, to be understood. In fact, Aristotle, one of the few genuine developmentalists in Greek antiquity, insists that the integrity of the knowledge with which we begin our investigations makes a difference in the outcome, in the end of the investigations. Thus he holds that understanding the nature of children is a necessary condition for educating them. It is true that "that which children are to be" is one beginning, and aids in determining the actions by which we strive to realize that aim. It is true also, and equally important, that "that which children are as children" also aids in determining the actions by which they are to be shaped. This is true, even though as children, their nature is incomplete relative to their ultimate nature. Aristotle says, "reason and intelligence are for us the end of our natural development, so that it is with a view to these ends that our engendering and the training of our habits must be regulated."[50]

The point that Aristotle makes again and again is that some things, as our original nature, are good in relation to what they may become and so are not absolutely good. Yet the fact remains that Aristotle was such a consummate functionalist that he had to insist on taking means into account in terms of ends, and of beginning with ends in whose terms means are chosen. For Aristotle, living is activity in quest of happiness, yet the activities on the way to happiness are means. Happiness itself is a kind of conduct that has no end beyond it. Living is conduct involving proximate means as well as conduct involving happiness as the ultimate end we seek. In a sense, we humble ourselves in choosing the means by which we live for the most part, even while we are striving to become happy. We live out our lives in actions that are less than happy as we seek happiness.

Aristotle's interest in the nature of childhood is apparent in Book VII of the *Politics* where he argues, "[children] up to the age of five, which it is not well to direct as yet to any study nor to compulsory labors, in order that they may not hinder the growth, should nevertheless be allowed enough movement to avoid bodily inactivity."[51] He continues by emphasizing the importance of play, saying that "the games must not be unfit for freemen, not laborious, nor undisciplined."[52] Aristotle's notion that growth is not to be hindered did not prevent him from holding also that children's games should be disciplined. This is another example of his position that development is natural, yet needs to be controlled by a tutor who possesses the virtues for whose sake children are being educated. It is true that we are compelled to recognize an original nature as a fact of animal existence. In human behavior the original nature is not to be hindered in its development, yet is to be disciplined by those who take control, who are prepared by their own self-discipline to have in mind the ultimate nature for the sake of which the original nature and later proximate natures exist. Each nature which comes into existence is an end of earlier natures considered as means; once realized, ends are turned into means for the sake of other natures, more nearly complete, more fully human.

As a craft, the poliscraft is the sort of activity that seeks an economy of means to realize its ends; yet we cannot be sure of the results until we have lived a complete life. As an investigation, it is the sort of activity that cannot be sure of its ends; we can only strive to determine which of the ends is the end for which all other activities are taken as means, and then proceed to test the ends by use of the means we have chosen. The investigation continues, becomes part of the craft; and the craft goes on and on. For Aristotle, the functionalism of thought and action is complete. Though is *of* action, ultimately, of the highest and best activity. Proximately, action requires human beings to take thought. Action in its distinctly moral sense is conduct; and conduct must strive to shape itself by cooperating with the highest principles which our moral and intellectual natures are capable of determining.

Chapter **4**

ORATORY AS CONDUCT IN CICERO AND QUINTILIAN

In our discussion of the idea of conduct in Cicero and Quintilian, the aim is to emphasize the sense in which they take oratory not only to be *grounded* in human conduct, but to *be* a kind of conduct. While Quintilian does not agree with certain features of Cicero's conception of oratory, the ground they share in common is more extensive and more important than their differences.

Cicero called Isocrates "the Master of all rhetoricians, from whose school, as from the Horse of Troy, none but leaders emerged."[1] In Cicero we find a continuation of the Greek tradition in poetry and oratory that one must be educated in right conduct and in good speech. The influence of Aristotelian ideas is brought to bear in Cicero's argument that orator and philosopher combined make the best orator.

We will begin with Cicero's description of an orator at work: "In an orator we must demand the subtlety of the logician, the thoughts of the philosopher, a diction almost poetic, a lawyer's memory, a tragedian's voice, and the bearing almost of the consummate actor."[2] A "finished orator" is a rare bird. "No rarer thing ... can be discovered among the sons of men," Cicero writes.[3] Even with nature's gifts, with practice, and with great striving, however, the orator knows that what he wants may be different from what he gets. "Those [most eminent orators] who had

learned from experience and knowledge of human nature understood that
. . . the fate of a speech was sometimes not sufficiently in accordance with
their wish."[4] Although wide experience and considerable knowledge are
necessary if one is to become a good orator, they are not sufficient to make
him a successful one. Cicero comes close to echoing the ancient wisdom in
the famous line of Aeschylus: "Man must suffer to be wise."[5] For Cicero, the
good orator is a wise man who will suffer from the uncertainty that is a
consequence of his wisdom.

The idea that the education of an orator is an education in right
conduct is a continuing theme in Cicero's *De Oratore.* Not only is it
implicit in much that Cicero says, but it is made explicit in two ways. First,
in certain references to poetry and history which characterize the orator as
a man of action; and, second, in his discussions of the relationships between the art of oratory and the knowledge needed by an orator. As an
example of the first, Cicero recalls the story of Phoenix and young Achilles
in Homer's *Iliad,* quoting the passage in which Phoenix says that he had
been charged with making Achilles "an orator and man of action too."[6] The
point of the story, Cicero insists, is that it reminds us that "in old days . . .
the same system of instruction seems to have imparted education both in
right conduct and in good speech."[7] To emphasize the necessity of conduct
for an orator, Cicero says that Aristotle is a fine philosopher for students of
oratory to read. It was he who not only "put the whole of his system of
philosophy in a polished and brilliant form," but also "linked the scientific
study of facts with practice in style."[8] This is why Philip asked Aristotle to be
Alexander's tutor, Cicero goes on, "to impart to him the principles both of
conduct and of oratory."[9] Cicero takes care to emphasize the importance of
the orator "possessing wisdom combined with eloquence,"[10] saying that
"the prize must go to the orator who possesses learning."[11] Cicero argues
against separating the education of the orator from that of the philosopher.[12] He thought it was the teachings of Socrates which "separated the
science of wise thinking from that of elegant speaking, though in reality
they are closely linked together."[13] Cicero goes on to say that Socrates'
teachings are the source of "the undoubtedly absurd and unprofitable and
reprehensible severance between the tongue and the brain."[14] Whenever
we sever the education of the orator from that of the philosopher, we have
one set of teachers to teach us to think and another set to teach us to speak.
It is obvious that Cicero wants thinking and speaking to be twin attributes
of the orator. To put it in another way, he thinks an orator should be a
philosopher.

Oratory is not a skill attained by learning the rules of the rhetoricians.
It is closer to a way of being in the world: the orator celebrates an ideal of
excellence by means of the orations he creates on the strength of wide

knowledge and large experience. "The genuine orator," Cicero writes, "must have investigated and heard and read and discussed and handled and debated the whole of the life of mankind, inasmuch as that is the field of the orator's activity, the subject matter of his study."[15] The clear suggestion here is that the orator, giving voice to the oration that he has created, must be in command of much more than "the *principles* of conduct and oratory," which Phoenix tried to teach Achilles, and which Philip wanted for Alexander. What the orator must do is test the meaning of those principles in his attempts to persuade. Striving to give "verbal expression to the thoughts and purposes of the mind in such a manner as to have the power of driving the hearers forward in any direction in which it has applied its weight,"[16] is the practical aim of the orator. At this point the relationship between the potential power of the orator and the virtues possessed by the orator becomes clear. It is necessary for the power to be combined with "integrity and supreme wisdom," Cicero points out, "and if we bestow fluency of speech on persons devoid of those virtues, we shall have put weapons into the hands of madmen."[17] Here is Cicero's statement of the classic conception of the orator as "the good man speaking well," espoused before him by Isocrates, and to be praised later by Quintilian. At the same time, it is the orator's reply to Socrates' criticism of rhetoric in the *Gorgias*. As we have seen, Cicero's orator is a philosopher no less than he is an orator. Better put, unless he is a philosopher of a certain kind he cannot be an orator of substance. "For my part," Cicero writes, "my present inquiry is not which system of philosophy is the truest but which is the most fully akin to the orator."[18]

It is important to notice at this point that Cicero is not saying that "truth" has no place in oratory. Rather he appears to have taken from Aristotle the idea that orators are like statesmen in that they work with probabilities rather than with certainties. They work with what Aristotle calls "actions done", (as well as those remaining to be done), whose subject matter "admits of variation."[19] He praises the "older masters" before Socrates who "used to combine with their theory of rhetoric the whole of the study and the science of everything that concerns morals and conduct and ethics and politics."[20] This is the "study and science" of those subject matters that belong to Aristotle's *Nicomachean Ethics* and *Politics*. The way to become an orator lies in the "close alliance between oratory and philosophy,"[21] and for this the orator needs "width of culture."[22]

Cicero's orator, then, is the one who has studied the subject matters taken into account in Aristotle's ethical and political writings. With Aristotle, he understands that "in doing the end cannot be other than the act itself: doing well is in itself the end."[23] We need to see that the orator not only understands this, but also conducts himself in such a way that he strives to do well. Put differently, the claim is that Cicero's orator must understand human experience in ways so that he can speak persuasively, and at the same time, be the kind of person who employs his orations to improve his own conduct as a member of a community of human beings in action.

The art of oratory is concerned with what is shared by human beings, "with the common practice, custom, and speech of mankind."[24] Indeed, Cicero claims that it is a serious mistake to depart from the language of everyday life and from "the usage approved by the sense of the community."[25] This is why Cicero finds that Aristotle's commonplaces are "common" in the sense that they are the "places" in ethical and political conduct around which human beings of experience gather, and "among which every line of argument might be found."[26] Commonplaces stand for the sense of the community, a sense that is based on the wisest and best the culture has brought to pass in its history. At the same time, what is common is the basis for "every line of argument." As Cicero sees Aristotle's commonplaces they are "what is known to us," rather than what is "knowable in itself," to use Aristotle's language.[27] As in Aristotle's student of ethics-politics, so in Cicero's student of oratory: "It is from knowledge that oratory must derive its beauty and fullness,"[28] yet oratory is not "within the grasp of exact knowledge."[29]

In his own way, then, Cicero is telling us that oratory belongs to the class of things which Aristotle called "variable things" rather than to the class of things Aristotle called "scientific knowledge."[30] Cicero's orator must have had experience of a certain kind in order to find commonplaces that are useful. If the orator "is a stranger to social intercourse, precedent, tradition, and the manners and disposition of his fellow countrymen, those commonplaces from which proofs are derived will avail him but little."[31] This is perhaps where Cicero comes closest to acknowledging the wisdom of Aristotle's idea that the man of principles acts not only by *conforming* to right principle, but by *cooperating* with right principle.[32] In any case, the right principles with which one may cooperate are to be found in our commonplaces, and only the person who has had the experience for which the commonplaces stand is capable of cooperating. The experience gained through striving is the context in which the orator tests his worth. Certain powers are "gifts of nature,"[33] and cannot be derived from art. While holding that "good abilities may through instruction become better," there are others so lacking in natural gifts that they "cannot enter the ranks of the orators."[34]

The ancient wisdom that had moved Plato to say that one gets virtue by divine dispensation[35] is acknowledged by Cicero: "Others there are . . . so completely furnished with the bounty of nature, as to seem of more than human birth, and to have been shaped by some divinity."[36] The kinship among natural talent, long experience in both the life and the studies which concern morals and conduct in one's community, and the common-places, is a necessary one: What the naturally gifted orator writes and speaks comes to one who has had a certain experience of life and study; and what he writes and speaks will *be* the "places" common to the community in which he has had the experience. Cicero puts it this way: "The truth is that all the commonplaces, whether furnished by art or by individual talent and wisdom ... appear and rush forward as we are searching out and surveying the matter with all our natural acuteness."[37] The need for the orator to give expression to the best that has been experienced by members of a community which prizes certain things in common is discussed in a passage by Cicero. There he says that the rules of the art of eloquence which are taught by professors of rhetoric are a help towards right knowledge.[38] He also says that "certain persons have noted and collected the doings of men who were naturally eloquent: thus eloquence is not the offspring of the art, but the art of eloquence."[39]

The orator needs not only to study the past conduct, but to learn how to conduct himself and to persuade others to conduct themselves in certain ways. This is why Cicero points to the *doings* of eloquent men, not just to their *sayings*. Thus, the origins of an orator's subject matter are to be found in human conduct, and the consequences of an orator's gifts, experience, and performance must *be* conduct of certain kinds. Cicero knows of the need for investigation, for taking the conduct of philosophers and of those practiced in statecraft as the context in which commonplaces are determined. There is another reason why the education and the conduct of an orator need to be a continuing investigation: This is the unknown fate of one's oration, which Cicero expresses as a kind of humility in the midst of uncertainty.[40] In this he has something in common with Plato's philosopher-charioteer who seeks true knowledge but finds his steeds lamed and broken-winged, and learns that he must settle for a semblance of Truth.[41] He also shares the wisdom that one swallow does not make spring[42] with Aristotle's practitioner of statecraft.

Now to Quintilian. In his *Institutes of Oratory,* the conduct celebrated in great poetry and advocated in great oratory is emphasized in the education of an orator. The idea that the education of an orator is an education in conduct is Quintilian's no less than it is Cicero's. Quintilian's awe of the ancients is made obvious in his discussion of language:

> A certain majesty, and, if I may so express myself, religion, graces the antique. Authority is commonly sought in orators or historians. ... Custom ... is the surest preceptor in speaking; and we must use phraseology, like money, which has the public stamp.[43]

In the preface to his work, he recalls the classic idea that the orator "cannot exist unless as a good man." And in the final book, he insists that "an orator, then, is a good man."[44] Quintilian is dedicated to the idea that the customs of conventional wisdom (his counterpart of Cicero's commonplaces) are the basis for a sound education. "Custom in speaking, therefore, I shall call the agreement of the educated; as I call custom in living the agreement of the good."[45] Like Cicero, he too recalls Homer's Phoenix, a master who was "excellent as well in eloquence as in morals; one who . . . may teach his pupil at once to speak and to act."[46] Yet Quintilian realized that while one's studies are necessary, they are far from sufficient conditions of his education.

Choosing nurses whose morality is beyond reproach should be an essential responsibility of a child's father, Quintilian writes. The child's nurses should not be allowed to speak in ungrammatical ways, although "to their morals, doubtless, attention is first to be paid."[47] This attention to children's morals aims to make a difference in the adult orator. He characterizes the "perfect orator" as "a thinker of the best thoughts and a speaker of the best language,"[48] and likens him to the fearless orator imagined by Virgil in addressing an angry populace, when "With words/He rules their passions and their breasts controls."[49] Here we have "a good man," Quintilian says, "skilled in speaking."[50]

Quintilian agrees with Cicero that the study of dialectics is useful in the education of an orator. Yet the moral part of philosophy is more important. It is not merely to *understand* these things that we study them, Quintilian says. Virtues such as justice, courage, temperance, and self-control are to be known not "by sound and name only." We are to *live* them. The true orator, "who has embraced them in his heart, and thinks in conformity with them, will have no difficulty in conceiving proper notions about them, and will express sincerely what he thinks."[51] What is more, Quintilian assures his readers that the orator need not commit himself to any specific philosophic sect; what the orator strives for "is of a loftier and better nature, since he is to be distinguished as well by excellence of moral conduct as by merit in eloquence."[52]

Quintilian puts us in mind of Cicero's claim that commonplaces give expression to conduct of a certain kind from which and for which orators speak, in writing that it is essential for an orator "to bear continually in mind, the noble deeds and sayings which are recorded of the great men of antiquity."[53] And the commonplaces may be less than true: like the assertions made in Aristotle's study of statecraft, they "admit of variation." As Quintilian puts it, "oratory does not always purpose [propose] to say what is true, but does always purpose [propose] to say what is like truth."[54] There is a sense of Cicero's uncertainty about the consequences of an oration in Quintilian's urging us to "aspire to the highest excellence,"[55] even though Quintilian refuses to promise that we shall become the best. He claims only that "we shall either attain the summit, or at least see many below us."[56] The thing for human beings to do is to strive for the best. Above all, it is necessary to do this, even though there is no promise of victory.

In fact, Quintilian argues that the widely held idea, that the object of oratory is to persuade, is an inadequate one.[57] To persuade, Quintilian says, is an aim not confined to orators. For example, money "has the power of persuasion," as does a beautiful person, or a "pitiable appearance."[58] "Oratory," he insists, "is the art of speaking well."[59] And, if this is the case, Quintilian continues, the ultimate end of oratory "must be to speak well."[60] To give this conception of oratory a context, Quintilian again reminds his readers that "a true orator must be, above all, a good man."[61] Thus art and morality are joined in the mind and character of the orator and in the oration that he produces.

In one passage, Quintilian writes of three divisions of rhetoric: art, artist, and the work.[62] The art is the know-how of speaking well; the artist is the orator who has acquired the art; and the work is good speaking. Against those who argue that the end of art is to persuade, Quintilian insists that speaking well does not require victory to attain the end of the art. "So it is the object of an orator to speak well," he holds, "for his art . . . consists in the *act,* and not in the result."[63] As in Cicero, there is no promise of victory for the true orator.

In one sense, then, an oration is a work of art. It is something produced, as a painting. Orations are written down, and sometimes published. Yet, for Quintilian, the orator is more like a dancer than a painter. In distinguishing among the kinds of arts, Quintilian refers to: (1) the theoretic, "such as *astronomy,* which requires no *act,* but is confined to a mere understanding of the matters that form the subject of it"; (2) the practical, whose object "lies in the act, and is fulfilled in it, leaving nothing produced from it . . . as *dancing*"; (3) the productive, "which attain their end in the execution of the work which is submitted to the eye . . . as painting."[64] Quintilian holds that oratory partakes of the theoretic, as when the orator restricts himself to contemplation; here he says that "the pleasure derived from knowledge is pure when it is withdrawn from action . . . and enjoys the calm contemplation of itself."[65] He holds, also, that oratory is similar to a productive art in the written speeches and historical compositions it produces.[66] Even so, "as its performance consists chiefly in the mere act, and as it is most frequently exhibited *in act,* [let it] be called an *active,* or a *practical* art."[67] In the passage where oratory is likened more to dancing than to painting or astronomy, Quintilian again emphasizes the sense that oratory is a kind of art whose nature is action: "*oratory* consists in act, for it accomplishes in the act all that it has to do."[68]

Now we can see that the activity of the orator is intimately connected to the oration produced. True oratory is a kind of action whose integrity consists of art-artist-oration so tightly woven together that it is possible to distinguish among them but not to separate them in action. Perhaps Quintilian's sense of oratory as a kind of action, rather than a set of skills or a complex technical apparatus, is not well-known to students of history of education because most discussions of Roman oratory emphasize the details of the curriculum in the education of an orator, pointing to its dependence on a written literature of poetry, history, and oratory. Of course Quintilian did not neglect the curriculum in his *Institutes*; in fact, that work is one of the most-quoted sources used by historians in reconstructing the education of an orator in Ancient Rome.[69]

In emphasizing Quintilian's conception of oratory as an active art, we are simply making plain two ideas that give more specific meaning to our earlier discussion of the true orator as the "good man speaking well." (1) The subject matters which contain the main body of commonplaces are *means* to the education of an orator, not ends in themselves. (2) This means that commonplaces become active in the education of an orator when they enter into the orator's life, when they become essential to his action rather than merely to his understanding and to his orations. In this sense, orations produced in action are a part *of* the action. Even though they may be written down and published, and may be used as examples providing commonplaces for orators-in-training, their distinguishing feature is the kind of act they are. Remember that in the act is its fulfillment. Again, "[oratory] accomplishes in the act all that it has to do."[70] The quality and meaning of the life the orator has lived and is living are expressed in the oration. Nothing else is needed for the good man, not even success in persuading those who hear the oration. Now this is a far thing from the conception of an orator merely as pleader, defender, persuader, or sophist. Rather, the oration is the test of the meaning of the orator's life. The very quality of an orator's existence is made public in the attempt to speak well.

With this conception of oratory before us, we can see that Quintilian's assertion that the oratory which he tries to teach "must be regarded as a *virtue*"[71] is another way of characterizing the art. Quintilian has in mind an old idea of virtue, that there is a kind of action which excels in the conduct that is peculiar to each species of creature, e.g., swiftness in the racehorse, strength in the lion. Human beings excel in two kinds of conduct, Quintilian holds: eloquence and reason.[72] Of course the two are related; as we have said, the true orator is a philosopher as well. Put differently, oratory is a virtue, a way of conduct by which the good man unites eloquence and reason.

Finally, it is important for us to see that Quintilian is not saying merely that the true orator understands virtues such as justice, courage, temperance, and self-control. Of course the quality of oratory is enhanced when the orator possesses these virtues. Yet Quintilian wants to make a further and more important claim: oratory itself *is* a virtue. In putting it this way Quintilian simply wants to say that oratory is a way of life. Oratory is not a "bag of virtues." Rather it is the virtue by which we strive to integrate eloquence and reason in doing justice to the best in our nature.

Chapter 5

CONDUCT IN JEWISH AND CHRISTIAN THOUGHT

Paideia is a difficult-to-translate word which epitomizes the meaning of classical education in ancient Greece.[1] Its counterpart in the classical education of ancient Rome is "humanitas."[2] In one sense *paideia* stands for an ideal: what kind of human being the educated person will be. In another sense, *paideia* stands for educational practice, which aims to achieve the ideal by a curriculum consisting of the classic poets in its early stages, and oratorical and philosophical studies in its advanced stages. As we have seen in the writers already considered, the ideal looks to human beings as responsible for shaping their own destiny, cast about as they are by events often beyond their control. Such humanism has no extranatural or other-worldly support. Humanism, then, is naturalistic, and human beings make and break themselves in the world of natural things, having no recourse to a world apart from nature. We may accept the idea that there is a necessity in things, according to which our lives will come into being and pass away, as Aeschylus' *Agamemnon* seems to suggest. Or, we may risk overstepping our natural limits by striving to alter the nature of the necessity, as Sappho and Polyxena appear to do. In either way of conducting ourselves, however-er, our actions contribute to the events which make history. That history is a natural one. In part we are made and in part we make ourselves in that history; or, rather, *as* that history. It is the only history we have and, for better and for worse, we cannot escape from it. Perhaps that is the most compelling sense of the necessity in things which has endured from ancient paideia and humanitas.

Our poets, orators, and philosophers have held humanistic naturalism in common, despite their differences from one another. Yet also existing in the world of ancient humanism and naturalism were the Jewish scriptures and traditions. Jews themselves were educated in the paideia of classical humanism. At the same time, the Jewish religion was otherworldly; its God was above space and time; and while God's power influences the world of human beings, the human and natural world is of less value than God.[3] For ancient Jewish thinkers, the question of the relationship between Jewish orthodoxy and Greek philosophy came to be significant. Early Christian thinkers, also educated in classical humanism, were moved to consider the relationship between the naturalistic humanism of the classical poets, philosophers, and orators, on the one side; and the word of God, on the other. Here we shall consider Philo of Alexander, a Jewish thinker (ca. 25 B.C. – ca. 40 A.D.); and two Christian thinkers, Clement of Alexandria (c. 150 – c. 220); and Augustine (354–430). Ancient Jewish and Christian thinkers accepted the necessity of ways of conduct no less than did the naturalistic and humanistic thinkers. In doing so, they established classic "otherworldly" conceptions of human existence which stood alongside and opposed the classic "this-worldly" conceptions of the poets, philosophers, and orators.

Philo was a master of interpreting scriptural texts as allegory. Essentially, this means that scriptural texts were "not saying what they are saying, but saying something different,"[4] as one student of Philo puts it. "Allegory is the direct opposite of the literal,"[5] he continues. On the question of the relationship of the studies of the classical schools to acquiring the wisdom of Jewish religion, we will see what Philo says in his work, *On Mating with the Preliminary Studies*. This is an interpretation of Genesis xvi. 1–6, which tells a story of Abraham, his wife Sarah, and her handmaiden Hagar. According to the story, Sarah was not bearing children to Abraham, and suggested that Abraham beget children from Hagar; Abraham slept with Hagar, and she conceived. The point of the story, Philo writes, is that we are not capable of receiving virtue "unless we have first mated with her handmaiden, and the handmaiden of wisdom is the culture gained by the primary learning of the school course."[6] In the allegory, Sarah is virtue, and Hagar is the introduction to virtue; before Abraham can mate successfully with virtue, he must mate with her handmaiden. Hagar, Philo writes, is "the mind which exercises itself on the preliminary learning," while Sarah is "the mind which strives to win the palm of virtue and ceases not till it is won."[7] In a sense, the term "mating" is a suggestive figure. Yet for Philo it is more than a figure, for learning is a kind of mating, an intimate relationship between the one who strives to learn and the object of the striving. As he says, "The art or science that is studied does seize and take hold of the learner and persuades him to be her lover, and in like manner the learner takes his instructress, when his heart is set on learning."[8]

Two things are worth noting here. First, the activity that is called for: "seizing," "taking hold," "persuading," are active verbs, calling for action as a necessary condition of learning. Second, the place of "heart": one must yearn for the object to be learned; the object calls for heart as well as mind. For mind to work most fully, one must have heart. Ultimately, when we express virtue as "the Good," the Good must be loved if we are to attain it. What the heart desires is love of the Good, Philo appears to say in this passage: "For what is sweet in toil is the yearning, the fervour, in fact the love of the good."[9]

We never know, to our hearts' satisfaction, the virtue which Sarah represents, although we can be sure that it is the highest virtue which human beings strive to attain. We must strive to gain a virtue that we do not possess, and yet we cannot know it unless we gain it. With this in mind, it is difficult to resist the temptation to compare Philo with Plato. We say this even though Philo subordinates philosophy to wisdom: "Just as the culture of the school is the bondservant of philosophy, so must philosophy be the servant of wisdom."[10] We may argue that, in his own way, Plato takes the activity of philosophy to be a means to the end of virtue-in-itself, or the Good. Of course, it is a mistake to identify the wisdom dramatized as Plato's Good with the wisdom which comes with taking in the "Ethereal Wisdom" of Philo's God. It is the case, however, that Philo, like Plato, emphasizes the striving and the yearning for virtue. Certain minds "which are by nature apt and take delight in Contemplation"[11] take in the Ethereal Wisdom, Philo thinks. In saying, "they see it and taste it and are filled with pleasure, being fully aware of what they feel, but wholly ignorant of the cause which produced the feeling,"[12] Philo puts us in mind of Plato's virtue-in-itself. In both writers, there is the suggestion of a greater cause, about which human experience has intimations and feelings, but which remains beyond the reach of human beings. Like Plato, Philo is better able to characterize the yearning to be wise than he is to let us know what wisdom is. By the language he uses in attempting to capture the meaning of wisdom in words, Philo shows us that he does not know it.

The following sentence reminds us of Pindar's prizing of the natural over that which is taught: "While that which is taught needs a long time, that which comes by nature is rapid, and, we may say, timeless; and, while the one has man as teacher, the other has God."[13] Pindar's nature, of course, did not have Philo's God as teacher. Nevertheless, Philo's idea that what is taught "needs a long time" shares with Pindar's athletes the agony of struggle without promise of victory. Like Plato and Pindar, who both show us the necessity of discipline for furthering the advantage which comes to those gifted by nature, and the difficulties they encounter in taking advantage of their gifts, Philo holds, "that which is morally excellent is hard or even impossible to find in a life of turmoil."[14] Thus "the timeless," coming from God, "is rapid" yet it too has difficult sledding in the world of nature inhabited by those who must learn from teaching. In the sense that the timeless, once given, cannot be taken away, it endures for all time; but while it dwells among mortals it must struggle to maintain itself as do the less fortunate, who must be taught. In the end, search as they might, the minds gifted by nature do not "succeed in finding anything by search respecting the essence of Him that is."[15] This is the necessity in things which those who seek to know God must accept. Again, taking in the Ethereal Wisdom, tasting it, seeing it, taking pleasure in it, are not to know its source. To be wise is not to know what wisdom is; to be good is not to know what goodness is.

Thus our inability to know God does not prevent us from being virtuous. Only in the struggle to free ourselves from a complete dependence on human things may we become virtuous. And to be virtuous is to be free. Indeed, only the good person can be free, Philo argues. He remembers Polyxena "as thinking little of death but much of her freedom."[16] The subject matter of the schools, together with the teachings of the classic philosophies, cannot make us good; at the same time, we must remember that they are wisdom's handmaidens, prerequisites to virtue. They help us to reason, Philo maintains. He holds that the souls of virtuous men must be "strongly fortified with a resolution firmly grounded on reason."[17] The sort of philosophy which Philo admires is one which does not separate thought from action. It is "a philosophy which sets its pupils to practice themselves in laudable actions, by which the liberty which can never be enslaved is firmly established."[18] Practicing "laudable actions" that are "grounded in reason" is the mark of virtuous human beings. Yet particular deeds may not continue and words may be forgotten, so to call one's behavior virtuous means that it is long-lasting, a habit of conduct. Thus Philo quotes from a letter of Calanus: "With us deeds accord with words and words with deeds. Deeds pass swiftly and words have short-lived power: virtues secure to us blessedness and freedom."[19] We hear an echo of Pindar's strivers for excellence, Plato's philosopher in quest of virtue-in-itself, and Aristotle's seeker of happiness in this sentence: "The glory of the philosopher rests upon achievements of virtue, freely willed by themselves, and these being what they are, immortalize those who practice them in sincerity."[20] In passages such as this one, philosophers receive high praise, even though the highest wisdom accessible to human beings needs something more than the naturalism and humanism of classical education.

Philo's dissatisfaction with naturalistic humanism as an adequate ground for wisdom was shared by Clement of Alexandria, one of the founders of Christian philosophy. It is not our purpose here to discuss Christian philosophy for its own sake, but to point to certain of its features that most directly influenced Clement's idea of education and conduct. Clement recognized Greek philosophy as the propaideia of Christian philosophy. Clement's propaideia stands to Christian wisdom as Philo's handmaidens stand to Jewish wisdom. As Werner Jaeger puts it, "Only the propaideia comes from man; the true paideia itself comes from God."[21] Plato had said in the *Laws:* "God is the pedagogue of the whole world."[22] Clement read Plato to be suggesting an essential proposition of the philosophic propaideia. It is as if Plato had recognized part of the larger truth which is made possible, not by philosophy alone, but by philosophy's meanings altered and perfected by divine providence. Philosophy teaches us, but in imperfect and incomplete ways. The true pedagogue is Christ, whose teachings enable men to fulfill their nature in a degree higher than any merely human teachings can do. As Greek philosophy gave expression to the highest cultural ideal to be found in human teachings, so Christian theology can give expression to the ideal of Christian culture.

In this context Clement discusses Christ as the educator of human beings, using the Scriptures for his text. The Bible, unlike philosophic texts, is not the result of a human search for truth, but contains truths revealed to human beings by God. It is important to understand that Clement conceives his work *Paedagogus* to be based on divine revelation, on the words of God revealed to men, rather than on human inquiry. His references to human sources, such as philosophic speculation, are employed when they are useful in clarifying or illustrating the meaning of the logos that came from the divine source. The humanism and naturalism of classical education, human striving in a natural world, are found wanting, and are superseded by divine initiative. The pride of Plato's philosopher, striving to gain virtue-in-itself, is replaced by the humility of the Christian, who believes that his imperfections take their place in a universe which is transcended by a perfect Being.

In his *Paedagogus*, Clement pursues the idea that the propaideia must be put behind one who aims to be a Christian. One must understand that a simple way of life, not one complicated by philosophical investigations, is to be exalted. As explained by the Scriptures, "We are the children," Clement says.[23] That is, full-grown Christian men and women, as well as their children, are called "children" by Christ. In the Gospels, Jesus called his disciples children;[24] in another place Christians are referred to as young birds;[25] in another, as young colts;[26] in still another, as lambs.[27] They are also called young suckling calves[28] and guileless and meek doves.[29] By referring to Christians as young ones, Jesus lets us know that "Children are those who look upon God alone as their father, who are simple, little ones, uncontaminated."[30] What Jesus encourages grown-up Christians to do is to imitate children and, as little children do with their earthly parents, to "devote themselves to the Father alone."[31]

In the Scriptures, Jesus discusses those who are children of grown-ups in ways which point to the childlike qualities which are most praiseworthy: "gentleness and simplicity of mind and guilelessness," Clement says, are praised "before all other qualities men can possess."[32] These qualities are found in the conduct of children. The simplicity of soul which belongs to childhood, Clement argues, is recommended by Jesus for our imitation. This is the meaning of the Lord's admonition, "Unless you turn and become like little children, you shall not enter into the Kingdom of Heaven."[33] Clement insists that these words are not a figure of speech for a kind of rebirth; they mean, in a direct way, that the simplicity of childhood is to be imitated. Clement also holds that Jesus "likened the Kingdom of Heaven to 'children seated in the marketplace'."[34] Again, Jesus said: "Let the little children be, and do not hinder them from coming to Me, for such is the kingdom of heaven."[35] Clement insists again and again that it is the youngest ones, in their innocence, who are most worthy of being imitated; he refers to their simplicity of mind in some places, their simplicity of soul in others. What adults need to learn is a conduct that is innocent, like that of children. They must put behind them the conduct taught in classical education.

Clement knows full well that the world of classical education looks upon such adoration of innocence as foolishness. He draws upon the conventional wisdom of the propaideia which defines education "as a sound training from childhood in the path of virtue."[36] It is clear, however, that Clement departs from the philosophic conception of virtues which insists that education is a process of growing away from simplicity and toward sophistication. Indeed, what Jesus teaches us is that the sophistication of the philosophers which we have learned must be overcome by imitating the nonsophisticated young ones, by becoming childlike. Christians must do this, if they are to enter the Kingdom of Heaven. This is something which Clement learned, not from philosophers, but from the divine logos. Thus Clement turns around the order of values in classical education. The sophisticated paideia, which educated Christians learned from the philosophers, is prior to the less sophisticated paideia of Christ the educator. But the former is inferior to the latter and, thus in its own way, its servant. In saying, "we also call the most excellent and perfect possessions in life by names derived from the word 'child,' that is, education and culture [paidagogis and paideia, from pais],"[37] Clement means to contrast the old classical paideia with the new Christian one. The old paideia held that the highest ideal of excellence is pursued by those minds who can learn to become disciplined in the pursuit of the best. The new paideia holds that the best ideal, the one most worthy of imitation, is to be found in the innocent simplicity of childhood. Clement found in childhood not a nature to be changed to a higher form, but a nature possessing qualities already worthy of being admired and imitated by grownups. To aim to realize our highest nature, we must try to imitate the virtues of children. The best examples of virtue among human beings, God's children on earth, are to be found in the natural innocence possessed by the youngest of them.

Clement contrasts "the world's" conception of the child with the one he is making explicit by saying that to lay aside the cares of life and give heart and mind to God will be taken by God in one sense and by the world in quite another sense. "Whoever fulfills this command is a little one, indeed, and a child, both before God and the world: to the world, in the sense of one who has lost his wits; to God, in the sense of one dearly beloved."[38] The world's sense that children are witless derives from the expectation that education should help children get their wits by becoming wiser in the ways of this world. The aim of humanistic and naturalistic education is sought in and among the things of this world. Philosophers of the world attempt to become larger in understanding. They aim to enlarge themselves, not to remain "little". By contrast, God loves the "little ones," for the very qualities the philosophers strive to overcome. The qualities that enable us to call them children stand in opposition to the prideful seekings of the philosophers; indeed, children are innocent of those kinds of seekings. What grownups should try to imitate in the little ones is simplicity rather than complexity; absence of worldliness rather than worldly-wisdom; little rather than large; meek rather than prideful.

To be a little one, however, is not to be lacking in intelligence. Clement distinguishes "childishness," which means lacking in intelligence, from "childlikeness," which means gentle, "decidedly amenable, mild and simple, without deceit or pretense, direct and upright of mind."[39] One who is childlike rather than childish tends to be simple and truthful, because he is "tender" and thus prepared to receive the Truth. The tenderness lies in being "guileless as to what is evil," while remaining "wise as to what is good."[40] To be likened to children who are simple and innocent is to be "one newly become gentle."[41] Such a person has put aside the values of the worldly-wise, and has left himself "open" in two ways: (1) to the criticism of the world, and (2) to receive the wisdom that is possible for one who has put aside worldly things and looks to the Lord for instruction. In one sense, *child* is reserved for those who are learning truly, and *man* is reserved for those who are "complete," i.e., complete in wickedness. To trust in the things of the world, then, is to leave oneself open to wickedness, open to becoming "man in the sense that he is consummate in wickedness."[42] From Clement's Christian perspective, one who is open to receive the things only an innocent one is capable of receiving is also open to the criticism of the world, because such a one is not willing to receive the things which make human beings "consummate in wickedness."

We see here a fundamental break from what Jaeger has called the propaideia of the philosophers, from the teachings of the poets, philosophers, and orators. It is a suspending of the values of this world in order to leave oneself open to the teachings of Christ. The aim is for us to regain the sort of innocence that we had as little children. It is not just that Christ teaches us different virtues from those of the philosophers. A more radical idea is proposed: what Christ teaches cannot be learned merely by adding his teachings to what philosphers teach us; it can only be learned by those who, like children, are naturally innocent, or by those who, like grown-up Christians, have newly become gentle, have laid aside "the cares of life and give[n] [their] whole mind and heart to the Father alone."[43] Only by doing this can one hope to become wise in the ways of the Lord.

So far we have spoken of a sense in which children live first of all, in innocence. This idea of childhood suggests a way of being that grownups must take on if they are to become wise according to the teachings of Christ rather than according to the teachings of the philosophers. Yet childhood has another meaning, one for which the teachings of the philosophers prepared Christians. The humanistic and naturalistic conception of education emphasized the eternal character of the highest ideal of culture. Plato sought virtue-in-itself, an unchanging eternal shape which ultimately remains impervious to understanding by human reason; yet proximately it is subject to the probings of reason, for all its ultimate incomprehensibility. For Plato, the activity of human reason in working towards the understanding it is capable of realizing does so by moving away from childhood, coming to terms with a higher kind of goodness, one to be understood in more and more mature ways during the course of inquiry. The eternal shape is an ideal which can be fully realized, if at all, only at the end of inquiry. What is eternal is known at the completion of the search, not at the beginning. Yet Christ the educator teaches us differently, according to Clement. The incorruptible, the eternal, is the childlike, not the mature. Christians are the *new people*; they must be new to partake of the Word of God. The *old people* have not been enlightened as Christians have. Inasmuch as Christians have looked to God's teachings and away from the teachings of the philosophers, they have learned from the *new Word*. Yet the new Word is eternal; to believe in it Christians are like children who are new to the world. In this sense, then, the eternal is with children who are innocent and guileless, rather than with those who have learned the ways of the world.

The reversal of the places of maturity and immaturity in Christian paideia is dramatized by Clement's insistence that the immaturity of childhood has a wisdom of its own. In one sense, childhood symbolizes a way of looking at the world that is the *new way* of Christian paideia, a way which is not only different from philosophic propaideia but is innocent of that paideia, or comes to one who puts that paideia behind him. At the same time, it must not be thought of as lacking in reason. "He does not mean by 'little child' one who has not yet reached the use of reason because of his immaturity, as some have thought."[44] Clement means that a little child has a reason of its own, not a reason expressed in the language and with the subject matters of the philosophers, but one which has its own way of being in the world. It is the sort of reason which is given expression through the divine logos and is revealed in the holy texts. The world it portrays consists of things not known to the world of classical humanism. Thus the rationality of the philosophic propaideia, mature in its own way, and explaining the wisdom of the "old people," is immature in reference to the Christian paideia, and lacks the fresh confidence that comes with the holy wisdom of the divine logos. Little ones have an innocence which, if possessed by grownups, would be a maturity for them, for it would mean that grownups had put aside the immaturity of philosophic wisdom and had prepared themselves to cultivate holy wisdom. In doing this, they may be able to look upon God as their father, even as children look upon their human fathers in a pure, direct, and simple way.

In one place, speaking of Christians, Clement says, "After we have repented of our sins, renounced our wickedness and been purified by baptism, we turn back to the eternal light, as children to their Father."[45] Quoting Luke 10:21, where Jesus remarks that his Father hid things from wise and prudent people and "revealed them to little ones,"[46] Clement insists that Jesus means that the little ones are more ready for salvation than are those who are wise in the ways of the world. Again, it is those innocent in the ways of the world to whom the highest things are revealed. That which is eternal appears to those immature as the little ones are, not to those mature in the ways of the world. Once more, the order of values found in the philosophic propaideia is reversed: there the innocent little ones were incapable of experiencing the best; wisdom came, if at all, to the worldly-wise. In Christian paideia, the innocent are the ones best prepared to receive the highest teachings; the worldly-wise have to *unlearn* what their reason and experience have taught them is the highest and the best by nature if they are to become innocent. Little ones have the advantage here, because they have nothing to unlearn; experienced ones have to learn to be innocent.

In his own way, Augustine contrasts the teachings of philosophers with "the commandments of the gods."[47] Some philosophers, Augustine writes, "established important points, insofar as they had divine assistance, while they went astray in so far as they were hindered by human weakness."[48] Divine providence made this possible, for two reasons which complement one another: (1) to restrain the pride of human beings, and (2) "to show, by contrast, the way of piety, which starts from humility and ascends to the heights."[49] Like Philo and Clement, Augustine points to the inadequacies of merely human discoveries in guiding human beings to virtue and blessedness, the insufficiency of human reason in gaining access to the highest truths, those of Christian doctrine. The discoveries of philosophers are the counterpart, in Augustine, of Philo's handmaiden to wisdom and of the philosophic propaideia which Clement recognized. The ordering of things according to divine providence is Augustine's counterpart of the teachings of Christ the pedagogue in Clement. Yet the *counterparts* are not identical: each emphasizes the propaideia in different ways, and what divine providence orders for Augustine is not exactly what Christ teaches Clement.

Among the philosophers, Augustine held the work of the Platonists in the highest regard. He was unable to accept completely the Platonists' ideas because they thought it was right to worship a plurality of gods. Even so, he held them to be superior to other philosophers, saying, "There are none who come nearer to us than the Platonists."[50] This is because of the nature of Plato's moral philosophy, in which Plato held that "the wise man is the one who imitates, knows, and loves . . . God, and that participation in this God brings man happiness."[51] A dimension of Aristotle's thought is evident in Augustine's version of Platonism, where Augustine discusses the *Summum Bonum* as follows: "To which we refer all our actions, which we seek for its own sake, not for any ulterior end, and the attainment of which leaves us nothing more to seek for our happiness. For this reason it is called the 'end'; everything else we desire for the sake of this, this we desire for itself alone."[52] Thus he joins Plato's quest for virtue-in-itself with Aristotle's quest for happiness.

Yet the thoroughgoing and unrelenting passion for conduct of a certain kind is clearly what Augustine found to be so appealing in Platonism. The desire to conduct oneself in a certain way is so apparent in Augustine's work that it is a kind of truism about human existence. In the passage, "if man has been so created as to attain, through the special excellence in man's being, to that excellence which is superior to all other beings, that is, to the one true God of supreme goodness, without whom no being exists, no teaching instructs, no experience profits,"[53] the aim is to attain, and the struggle in human existence is in the striving to attain. While it is obvious that Augustine's "one true God" is different from Plato's virtue-in-itself and from Aristotle's happiness, it is also clear that Augustine shares with them the belief that it is in the striving to enjoy the highest end of human existence that our integrity is gained, our highest possible nature realized.

In his work, *On Christian Doctrine,* the aim is to teach Christians how to study the Scriptures, and to provide specific recommendations as to the ways in which Christians are to make use of classical humanistic writings. Augustine makes it clear that the way to Wisdom is conduct of a certain kind. There he sets forth seven steps, beginning with fear and ending with Wisdom.[54] "Before all," he writes, "it is necessary that we be turned by the fear of God toward a recognition of His will."[55] Fear will enable us to think of our mortality, of our future death, and will restrain our pride. From fear "we become meek through piety,"[56] the second "step of knowledge"; it is a piety by which we can humble ourselves by believing that what is written in the Scriptures is better and more true than anything we can think by ourselves. Piety prepares us for lamentation, for fear and piety, by which the Christian understands and acknowledges his own situation, "will force him to lament his own situation."[57] After lamentation the next step is fortitude, in which he has the strength to hunger and thirst for justice. Notice that such "steps," or "affections of the spirit," are not states of mind passively held, but are actions in quest of Wisdom. Take this sentence as an example, which is both a celebration of, and an appeal to, action: "And by means of this affection of the spirit [fortitude] he will extract himself from all mortal joy in transitory things, and as he turns aside from this joy, he will turn toward the love of eternal things, specifically toward that immutable unity which is the Trinity."[58] With fortitude, which enables him to see the Trinity "glowing in the distance," the Christian comes to the fifth step, "the counsel of mercy."[59] In mercy, one exercises the love of his neighbor; "when he arrives at the love of his enemy"[60] he ascends to the sixth step. Here he cleanses the eye through which he may come to see God. It is necessary "to die to the world as much as they are able" in order for the light of the Trinity to appear to Christians.

Here we see a counterpart of Clement's childhood innocence which enables children to see things that the philosophers do not see. Christians who are older than children, aged by the steps to Wisdom, must learn to do what Clement's innocents are able to do. "This holy one" (who has cleansed his eye), Augustine says, "will be of such simple and clean heart that he will not turn away from the Truth either in a desire to please men or for the sake of avoiding any kind of adversities to himself which arise in this life."[61] What one who has reached the seventh step to Wisdom is capable of seeing and doing is akin to what Clement's innocent ones are capable of seeing and doing: by unlearning the ways of the world, one becomes innocent of them. Yet it is clearly an agony of existence, through an experience of conduct, that we become innocent. (By comparison, Clement's guileless little ones had an easy time of it.) The seventh step is Wisdom, "where he enjoys peace and tranquility."[62] The subject matters of this world are useful to Christians insofar as they are means to Christian ends. Proximately, they may be helpful in understanding the Scriptures; while, ultimately, understanding the Scriptures is a means by which we try to conduct ourselves to the highest end, Wisdom. And only Wisdom is an end in itself, rather than a means to a further end.

The kind of conduct Augustine sees children engaged in, together with their original nature as set forth in the Scriptures, constitutes the context in which he spells out their nature. Augustine emphasizes the ignorance, the suffering, and the inescapable burden which Adam's sin has put on all human beings, and children are not spared. Augustine believes that we are dependent on divine grace, "not for philosophy of any kind, but for the true philosophy."[63] And what is more, "from this life of misery, a kind of hell on earth, there is no liberation save through the grace of Christ our Saviour, our God and our Lord."[64] Clearly, then, the pride of human beings in their merely human undertakings is a condition from which we must escape; the value of pride lies more in the "restraint" which it teaches us. We must restrain ourselves from supposing that we can escape the crimes of human society by our activities alone. Yet, even in humility, a virtue superior to the misplaced hopes which the pride of philosophers leads us to have, we cannot be assured that we shall enter the Kingdom of Heaven. Only by God's grace may we do that. As we have seen in outlining the seven steps to Wisdom, humility is a necessary condition of Christian education which we have to learn in order to overcome pride, a condition of the philosophic education. Even so, humility is a merely human condition, and is not sufficient in itself to overcome the ignorance which is endemic to the human condition, shared by all the children of Adam.

Not only the crimes of the most wicked men, but the sins of children "spring from that root of error and perverted affection which every son of Adam brings with him at his birth."[65] In referring to his own childhood in the *Confessions*, Augustine said that he had been "so small a boy and so great a sinner."[66] Augustine could not remember his infancy, but he had observed infants and believed he saw in them what he had been. The innocence of infants, Augustine held, is in their limbs, not in their wills.[67] He says that he had seen a baby envious; even though it could not speak, "it turned pale and looked bitterly on its foster brother."[68] He reminds us that we tolerate behavior in infants which would be intolerable in an older person. Augustine takes many opportunities to let his readers know that infant behavior is tolerated, not because infants are lacking in sin but because they are incapable of knowing what they are doing.

As Augustine reached boyhood, he learned to speak; in speaking, he gave expression to his will in a different way. The power of speech led him deeper into the trials of human life. He prayed to God that he not be beaten at school; not only was he beaten, but his parents mocked his beatings.[69] He later came to understand that the Lord spared him from folly, in permitting him to be beaten. It is folly for a child to transgress the commands of his parents and schoolmasters, even though parents and masters themselves act foolishly. Even so, the Lord used such errors for Augustine's good: "By those who did not well, Thou didst well for me; and by my own sin Thou didst justly punish me."[70] He makes essentially the same point in *The City of God*, when he writes:

> For what is the meaning of the manifold fears which we use on little children to keep their foolishness in order? What is the purpose of the pedagogue, the schoolmaster, the stick, the strap, the birch, and all the means of discipline? By such means, as holy Scripture teaches, the flanks of a beloved child must be beaten, for fear he may grow up untamed, and become so hardened that he is almost or even completely, beyond discipline. What is the point of these punishments, but to overcome ignorance and to bridle corrupt desire—the evils we bring with us into the world?[71]

At one place in his *Confessions,* Augustine writes as if he is arguing against a Clement-like conception of childhood innocence. After citing a long list of transgressions remembered from his childhood, including lies, love of play, petty thefts, desire of pre-eminence over his playmates, Augustine asked, "And is this the innocence of boyhood?" He cried out this reply: "Not so, Lord, not so."[72] The sins of childhood, he goes on to say, are transferred from the elders of childhood such as parents and schoolmasters to the elders of adulthood such as magistrates and kings, as one becomes older. The sins of childhood are but earlier versions of the sins of the latter. It should be obvious that, though smaller than adult sins, childhood sins are important in the eyes of the Lord, and so should be recognized as such by the child's earthly teachers.

Clement has referred to Jesus' statement, "Let the little children be, and do not hinder them from coming to Me, for of such is the Kingdom of

Heaven,"[73] as the highest of praises. For Clement, Jesus means that little ones are worthy of imitation because their simplicity of mind and guilelessness are qualities to be praised "before all other qualities men can possess."[74] In decided contrast, Augustine writes, "It was the low stature then of childhood, which Thou our King didst commend as an emblem of lowliness, when Thou saidst, Of such is the Kingdom of Heaven."[75] Thus Augustine sees the sins of children as less severe than those of adults, as manifestations of the "low stature" of childhood. To put it differently: in the less severe sinfulness of childhood there is to be seen something of the Kingdom of Heaven; for all its sins, childhood is the emblem of lowliness among sinners. We may say that, while children, like adults, are sinners they are lesser sinners.

In the work, *On the Merits and Forgiveness of Sins, and On the Baptism of Infants,* written in opposition to the doctrines of the Pelagians, Augustine wrote at length on the meaning of infant sin. Pelagius had written, "Nothing that is good and evil, on account of which we are either praiseworthy or blameworthy, is born with us—it is rather done by us; for we are born with capacity for either, but provided with neither."[76] This is an explicit denial of Augustine's doctrine that, because of Adam's sin, all of his successors are born corrupted. For Pelagius, the idea that nothing good or evil is born with us means that "there is no original sin in infants at all."[77] Pelagius' idea that we become good or evil, rather than being born either way, has certain affinities with Clement's idea of childlike innocence, yet is not identical with it. To be neither good nor evil, to be *innocent* of both, is to lack any particular quality. Clement's innocence seems to be a good in itself; it is innocence of evil, yet characterized by a simplicity of soul, lacking sophistication in the ways of the world but thereby possessing a certain presence, a kind of integrity of soul. What Clement and Pelagius do share is the idea that children are not sinful in their beginning. Their innocence is of will as well as of limb.

We have seen that Augustine argues, in the *Confessions,* that infants are not free from sin, that they are innocent only in limb. This means that certain activities which are tolerated by their elders are not innocent, but are due to a corruption of their nature as a consequence of Adam's sin. Thus Augustine can detect sin in infants' activities as soon as one can say that their wills are being expressed. In his anti-Pelagian treatise, Augustine makes a distinction between (1) the sins of very young infants, "new born babies," and (2) those of children who are learning to speak and are old enough to know their mothers and fathers.[78] It is regarding the newborn infants that he is most concerned with refuting the Pelagians' point of view, in order to establish the inescapability of holding to the doctrine of original sin. The evil in newborn infants is in their ignorance; it is their ignorance which needs to be corrected. This is the meaning of the prayer in Psalms XXIV:7, "Remember not the sins of my youth and of my ignorance," Augustine says.[79] That sentence would not have been necessary if there were no sins of ignorance, Augustine continues.[80] Thus infants do not knowingly commit their sins and hence are less to be condemned than older people who sin knowingly. This is a restatement of the point made earlier, that the lowly status accorded children among sinners is due to the lesser importance of their sins. Again, Augustine points out the mistake of those who call infants innocent, providing the following as evidence of sin implanted in them: "their great weakness of mind and body, their great ignorance of things, their utter inability to obey a precept, the absence in them of all perception and impression of law, either natural or written, the complete want of reason to impel them in either direction."[81] Incapable of learning how to sin, very young infants must have had the ability originally; it is natural to them as successors of Adam.

Augustine uses his observations of infants and children as illustrations of truths of Christian doctrine. What he takes to be palpable facts, ubiquitous in their manifestation, are already facts of Christian doctrine. If a Pelagian were to say to Augustine: "I see what you point to: a small child crying and looking bitterly at someone. But 'looking bitterly' is a figurative expression to suggest what an older person would do; the child, being ignorant of bitterness, cannot really be bitter, though he may 'look' bitter. Thus the fact that the child is crying and looking a certain way is not to be disputed. What is disputed is your interpretation of this as a 'fact of sin'." To this, Augustine might reply as follows: "The child's activities are sinful, not because of its knowledge of sin, but because its nature is corrupted by original sin. What I see is not just a child crying and looking a certain way, but a child sinning, even though it is incapable of knowing what it is doing. Indeed, its sinning is a sign that it needs to be purged of its natural weakness. What you call my 'interpretation' is a fact, an illustration of the truth conveyed in the prayer, 'Remember not the sins of my youth and of my ignorance.'"

It is obvious that Augustine does not find in childhood an innocence that is worthy of imitation. Instead, we first sin out of ignorance and later we sin knowingly. Even so, Augustine finds something to admire in children, a kind of integrity in the midst of childhood sinning. In concluding the discussion of his own boyhood in the *Confessions,* Augustine writes:

> For even then I was, I lived, and felt; and had an implanted providence over my own well-being,—a trace of that mysterious Unity, whence I was derived;—I guarded by the inward sense the entireness of my senses, and in these minute pursuits, and in my thoughts on things minute, I learnt to

> delight in truth, I hated to be deceived, had a vigorous memory, was gifted
> with speech, was soothed by friendship, avoided pain, baseness, ignorance.[82]

Human beings are capable of taking on certain virtues, such as truthfulness
and friendship, and of avoiding certain vices. Indeed, Augustine adds to his
earlier remark about himself as a boy, "so small a boy and so great a
sinner," a counterpart: "in so small a creature, what was not wonderful, not
admirable?"[83] While children are all-too-human and cannot avoid sinning,
they are capable of taking on a certain congruity or harmony with things, a
kind of *oneness* in the midst of their sinful behavior. In fact, whatever
integrity they gain must come into being in the midst of their sinfulness; it
cannot be otherwise for they are sinful by nature. However, we cannot
attribute much to this-worldly human abilities to gain virtuousness. Augustine holds that whatever virtues he learned as a boy "are gifts of my God; it
was not I, who gave them me."[84] It is human to sin. It is also human to
receive the gifts from God which give us integrity. "These [gifts] together
are myself," Augustine adds.[85] For Augustine, then, the idea of childhood
suggests not an innocence with an integrity of its own to be imitated, but a
sinful way of being that can take on an integrity which is wonderful and
admirable though not innocent. And God has given him whatever makes
him the kind of person he is, so Augustine thanks God and prays to him that
he might preserve the gifts, and prays further that he will enlarge and
perfect them.

Our reading of Clement and Augustine shows us that their responses
to the same Christian attribute of childhood are fundamentally different. In
childhood innocence, Clement finds an ideal in which those who are less
innocent may see a prospect for their own behavior. For Clement, innocence is good, a way of being in the world that others might learn. By
contrast, Augustine does not recognize children as morally innocent creatures; he finds sin in their behavior; the conduct of children is not to be
taken on by grownups. Finally, they share this belief with Philo: humanistic
and naturalistic paideia is the handmaiden, the propaideia of the highest
wisdom. At the same time, they share with this-worldly poets, orators, and
philosophers the belief that the integrity of human beings is to be determined only in conduct rather than in intellectual activity apart from conduct.

Chapter **6**

JOHN OF SALISBURY'S DEFENSE OF THE ARTS

The Metalogicon, the twelfth century work of John of Salisbury, is a Christian defense of the arts of verbal expression and reasoning. John's exposition and defense of the arts is with an eye to conduct. He puts it this way in the Prologue: "I am convinced that all things read or written are useless except so far as they have a good influence on one's manner of life. Any pretext of philosophy that does not bear fruit in the cultivation of virtue and the guidance of one's conduct is futile and false."[1] John, like his favorite poets, orators, and philosophers, strives to put the technical apparatus involved in speaking and thinking to the end of improving human conduct.

Whatever gifts we have by nature, John argues, they cannot be "fully realized without study."[2] He quotes this passage from Horace:

I neither see what study can do in the absence of natural talent, nor what natural talent can accomplish without cultivation, so much does one demand the assistance of the other, and so closely do they cooperate.[3]

He goes on to say that nature may "with the aid of virtue . . . grow strong."[4] This is a counterpart of Pindar's sense that we must take with good grace what the gods give us and, by striving, find out what we can become. At one point, John writes of the striving for virtue as if it is a kind of contest by which human beings are capable of overcoming nature: "It is a wonderful thing to see virtue victorious over nature."[5] While, for the most part, John argues that our study and our work are done in cooperation with nature, in this line he suggests that there is something in our nature that we must overcome if we are to become virtuous. In arguing that the art of eloquence is not known by nature, but is acquired by study and work, John says: "It is imprudent to expect of nature, without human assistance, that which is chiefly the work of man."[6] Again, in emphasizing the "*work* of man," John places the responsibility for the quality of human conduct on human activity; we cannot blame nature for that which is not natural; the outcome of our activity results from our work in cooperation with our nature, not from our nature alone.

The usefulness of logic is emphasized in what John calls its broadest sense, "the science of verbal expression and reasoning," and in a narrower sense, when it is "limited to rules of reasoning."[7] He goes on to say that "all logic is both useful and necessary."[8] Indeed, to understand that logic is an art is to place it among "the arts of doing all things that we are to do."[9] Thus the meaning of the idea that the art of eloquence is due to the work of man is generalized to take in all the "arts of doing." Another idea, that nature requires human assistance in the work of man, is cast again in John's characterization of art as "a system that reason has devised in order to expedite ... our ability to do things within our natural capabilities."[10] Reason, John continues, "substitutes for the spendthrift and roundabout ways of nature a concise, direct method of doing things that are possible."[11] While "nature is the mother of all the arts,"[12] human reason is needed to develop them. In sum, we may say that human reason, with the arts it develops, enables us to do what is not possible by nature alone. While John appears to find nature's ways to be more "roundabout," "wasteful," and "circuitous"[13] than does Aristotle, in principle he agrees with Aristotle that "generally art partly completes what nature cannot bring to a finish, and partly imitates her."[14] John's treatment of grammar points to the imitative function of art: "While grammar has developed to some extent, and indeed mainly, as an invention of man, still it imitates nature, from which it partly derives its origin."[15] By this John means that the things about us were formed first by nature, then were named and described by human beings in order that they might discourse with one another about them and with them. Thus while it is natural that human beings name and describe things and talk with one another about them, the precise nature of the arts employed is developed by the activity of human reason. An intimate and substantial way in which art imitates nature is spelled out in John's idea, following Horace, that "the rules of poetry clearly reflect the ways of

nature,"[16] meaning that "a poet must never forsake the footsteps of nature."[17] Two matters are apparent in these ideas: "reflecting the ways of
nature" and "never forsaking the footsteps of nature," and are to be seen in
his quoting of the following lines from Horace:

> Nature first adapts our soul to every Kind of fate: she delights us, arouses our
> wrath, Or overwhelms and tortures us with woe, After which she expresses
> these emotions employing the tongue as their interpreter.[18]

First is nature's preparation of the soul to take on the interpretations of the
poet. Second is the sense of activity implicit in nature's "ways" and "footsteps"; what nature calls for is action in the soul of the poet.

John's insistence that custom is "the supreme arbiter of speech"[19] is a
kind of counterpart of the importance which Aristotle and Cicero attach to
commonplaces. In the practice of speaking according to custom we cannot
be assured that we will speak the truth, yet only in striving to adapt our
speech to proper usage may we hope to speak the truth. His idea that only
the learned are capable of departing from customary usage[20] suggests that
there is a common ground, given by nature, which speech is capable of
comprehending and discussing; yet only those who are familiar with the
common can depart from it with integrity and strive to establish a different
custom. "What usage condemns," John writes, "cannot be reinstated save
by usage."[21]

In agreeing with Seneca that liberal studies do not make one good,
John means that "those who are merely philosophers are not good men."[22]
While holding that "it is charity alone that makes one good,"[23] he adds that
language, history, and poetry contribute "to the formation of virtue,"[24] and
agrees with Quintilian that studies are not harmful in themselves, but only
harm "those who become bogged down in them."[25] Again, he agrees with
Aristotle's predecessors, with Aristotle, and with the Roman orators that,
while the arts are not sufficient to make one virtuous, they are a necessary
condition of virtue. Human beings are not born good; whatever virtue they
take on comes to them through the actions they take. Another way he puts
the same point is to say that "scientific knowledge . . . must precede the
practice and cultivation of virtue."[26] John turns to I Corinthians 9:26 for the
happy expression that virtue "does not 'run without knowing where it is
going'."[27] While "grace alone can make one good,"[28] the seed of virtue is
planted by the arts, by which human beings become learned and practiced
as they take action in striving to do "good works." We might say that, for
John, the seed of virtue is that by which we aim to do good works. If we
succeed in doing them we "are called and actually are 'good'."[29] For our
purposes, the lesson is plain. Like Plato's philosopher in quest of virtue-in-

itself, and like Aristotle's poliscraftsman striving for happiness, the nature of integrity gained is found out in the action of seeking. It is better said that the integrity *is* the very quality of the action. For John, good works are not to be separated from activity. And "the love of what is good and the practice of virtue,"[30] the fruit of wisdom, are an inseparable activity: "loving" and "practicing" are modes of conduct. Together, they are a single activity.

John honors Aristotle as the "principle founder" of the art of logic, for it was he who organized logic "into a scientific art."[31] John follows Aristotle and Boethius in distinguishing between demonstration and "probable logic."[32] "Demonstrative logic," he points out, "rejoices in necessity," and "its sole concern is that a thing must be so."[33] Probable logic treats propositions which only "seem to be valid."[34] It deals with propositions that are "best known and most probable."[35] As arts, both dialectic and rhetoric are included in probable logic. It is these, along with grammar, that are most useful in affecting conduct. While dialectic "makes inquiry into the truth,"[36] its value to a disputant becomes clear when we recognize that the disputant needs to "establish with conviction what he is trying to prove."[37] It is the substance of the argument, "what is said,"[38] rather than the way it is said, which dialectic treats; it strives to establish the meanings of the words that are involved in argumentation. "A word's force consists in its meaning,"[39] John writes, and adds that "meaning breathes life into a word."[40]

Taken altogether, grammar, dialectic, and rhetoric combine and inquire into the meanings of words with ways of saying them that aim to persuade others that one course of action is the "most probable" among various courses of action. Logic aims to produce a "craftsman" in logic.[41] At the same time, such a craftsman aims to be something akin to Aristotle's poliscraftsman, a *Christian craftsman* aiming to gain Christian virtue in joint investigations and disputations with others. The *practical* or *active* sense of logic, along with its futility in the absence of wisdom or the lack of a grounding in commonplaces, is insisted upon again and again. At one point John quotes Cicero's statement that "Eloquence without wisdom is futile,"[42] adding that it should not be divorced from other studies. And in a well-known passage in which John tells of the disputatious dialecticians who had not engaged in other studies, and in whose hands dialectics lay "powerless and sterile," he concludes, "If it is to fecundate the soul to bear the fruits of philosophy, logic must conceive from an external source."[43] That John had fully grasped the significance and the difficulty of the instrumental function of the arts in cultivating virtue and doing good works is put in this way: "It is easy for an artisan to talk about his art, but it is much more difficult to put the art into practice."[44]

What has been said earlier in regard to John's general ideas about the aim of aiding nature to grow strong by the work of human beings employing the arts has now been confirmed in John's more specific discussions of logic. Not only are the arts in themselves crafts in the sense that they must be *practiced*; at the same time, if practiced in ways that employ external sources, they aim to lead to good works, to improved conduct.

In an interesting way, John's characterization of prudence combines Cicero's idea of it as having as its object "the investigation, perception, and skillful utilization of the truth,"[45] with Aristotle's discussion of the way the mind strives to apprehend universals by induction.[46] The subject matter of prudence is truth, John says.[47] He appears to have in mind two kinds of truth, one that is characteristic of probable logic, and another that is characteristic of demonstrative logic. As to the first, he treats prudence as if it is the sort of virtue which Aristotle treats in the *Nicomachean Ethics*, saying "prudence looks to the future, and forms providence, recalls what has happened in the past, and accumulates a treasury of memories; shrewdly appraises what is present, and begets astuteness or discernment; or takes full cognizance of everything, and constitutes circumspection."[48] What is this but a Christian version of Aristotle's prudence, an application of probable logic to various activities of human conduct? It is a recognition that the virtue of prudence has truth for its subject matter; yet it is the truth of probable logic, not of demonstration.

At the same time, and this is John's second kind of truth, he continues by suggesting that prudence is capable of attaining the kind of principles which are intuited by induction, the unproved premises of proof which constitute the universals necessary for a demonstrative science. For he adds to the passage just quoted, "and when it has ascertained the truth, prudence develops into a form of scientific knowledge."[49] In doing this, he recollects his earlier discussions of Aristotle's *Posterior Analytics,* in which the way of intuiting universals is set forth. John puts it in this way: "Many sensations ... result in a memory, many memories in an experimental proof, many experimental proofs in a rule, and many rules in an art which provides scientific skill."[50] Now for Aristotle, what John calls an "experimental proof" is "experience," and what John calls a "rule" is a "universal," which can stand as a first principle in demonstrative logic. Thus John combines probable logic, which we have found in so much of his discussion of the arts, with demonstrative logic, in such a way that he appears to strive for certainty amidst uncertainty or, better put, amidst probabilities. He takes probable logic to be capable of preparing the way to know the kind of principles that are needed in demonstrative logic. John presses opinion, learned from probable logic, to put us on the way to certainty. He does so in the following way. First he writes, "since human affairs are transitory, only rarely can we be sure that our opinion about them is correct."[51] Then he goes on to write of positing "as a certainty something that is not in all respects certain,"[52] adding that this is the "domain of faith," and claiming, "Faith is, indeed, most necessary in human affairs, as well as in religion."[53] Now it turns out that, in addition to opinion and science, the first determined by probable logic, the second by demonstration, John adds "faith" to his repertory of conduct in human affairs. "Faith is intermediate between opinion and science,"[54] John says, meaning that, like science, it affirms something with certainty, yet this certainty has not been determined by science. He quotes Hugh of St. Victor: "Faith is a voluntary attitude concerning something that is not present."[55]

Thus while Aristotle is John's first authority in matters of conduct bearing on opinion and science, he turns to the Scriptures and to Christian philosophers for faith, the third form of conduct. It is clear that faith, no less than the logics of inquiry and demonstration, requires action: each in its own way affirms something, the need to strive for opinion or certainty. Each also demands ways of conduct by which the nature of that which is affirmed is brought to pass.

Aristotle's *Nicomachean Ethics* and *Politics* were not available to John. What were available were Aristotle's writings on logic as well as his *Physics*. Thus while John shares Aristotle's sensitivity to the probable character of conduct as portrayed in poetry and oratory, his interest in making a science out of human ethical and political affairs led him to apply Aristotle's logic to those affairs in ways that Aristotle did not do. John made logic do for human conduct what Aristotle thought the subject matters of the poliscraft were not capable of doing.

This is not to say that John lacked caution in his approach to prudence. In the following lines, he writes with an Aristotle-like attention to the uncertainties in human conduct: "Handicapped as it is by errors begotten by sense perceptions and opinions, human prudence can hardly proceed with [entire] confidence in its investigation of the truth, and can scarcely be [completely] sure as to when it has comprehended the latter."[56] That is why John says that prudence must turn to "reason," whose estimate is "sure and reliable."[57] By this he means the kind of reason which argues from established principles to unmistakable conclusions. Reason, in this sense, is "both a power and the activity of a power."[58] Reason here is that activity in human beings nearest to divine reason; in a suggestive way of putting it, John says that such reason "is a virtual rather than a quantitative part of the Divine Spirit."[59]

We are able to see that John's quest for certainty, his desire to make a demonstrative science of prudence, departs from Aristotle's insistence that the subject matters of the poliscraft are not susceptible to being treated as demonstrative sciences. While Aristotle maintained that the end of the poliscraft was in the action undertaken by the participants in the craft, and not something to be formed that would stand apart from the action, John wanted to have it both ways: (1) in the sense that the means to the end are a way of conduct; and (2) in the sense that the end, a rule of conduct, stands apart from the conduct by which the rule was established. Thus John's Christian passion for certainty led him to depart from Aristotle's patience amidst the uncertainties of human beings striving for happiness. This led him to require a faith in a kind of outcome in human conduct which, for Aristotle, was not true to the nature of human beings striving for the highest excellence of which they are capable. For Aristotle, the action itself is the end; for John, in action we strive for an end that is capable of standing apart from the action.

Chapter 7

JOHN LOCKE AND ISAAC WATTS: UNDERSTANDING AS CONDUCT

John Locke yearned to make a demonstrative science out of the subject matters of conduct. Yet in his writings on ethics, politics, and education his common sense realism and his reliance on conventional wisdom remind us of the importance Cicero attached to commonplaces and of Aristotle's way of considering matters of prudence. At the same time, Locke was a Christian whose rationalism and belief in the possibility of improving human affairs did not stand in the way of affirming the existence of revealed truths that were not acquired by natural reason. Locke's thinking on conduct is explored here by examining (a) his conceptions of knowledge and judgment; (b) the relation between these and what Locke called "the skill of right applying our own powers and actions" in education; and (c) the place of revelation in conduct. As an example of an eighteenth century writer who shared Locke's thinking on conduct, we also discuss Isaac Watts' writings on logic and education.

When one examines Locke's attack on the doctrine of innate principles and the doctrine which Locke offers as an alternative, the limits of his empiricism, together with the hold which rationalism had on his mind, become apparent. He begins his criticism of the doctrine of innate principles by saying that ideas we have in our minds are not stamped there "in their very first being." Rather, the materials of reason and knowledge come from experience: "In that all our knowledge is founded, and from that it ultimately derives itself." Locke continues: "Our observation, employed either about *external sensible objects, or about the internal operations of our minds perceived and reflected on by ourselves is that which supplies our understandings with all the materials of thinking.*"[1] Locke elaborates on the above-mentioned either-or by using the figure, "fountains" of experience. One fountain which experience furnishes is *sensation,* by which the senses convey into the mind that which produces perceptions of ideas we call "yellow," "white," "heat," "cold," "soft," "hard," and the like. The second fountain Locke calls *reflection,* a perception of the operations of our own minds within us, producing ideas we call "thinking," "doubting," "reasoning," "believing," and the like.

For Locke, knowledge consists in *"the perception of the connexion and agreement, or disagreement and repugnancy, of any of our ideas."*[2] Locke means that when the mind perceives, when "a man infallibly knows,"[3] that the idea he calls black is not the idea he calls white, he perceives the disagreement between black and white. Or that, when one knows by demonstration that the three angles of a triangle are equal to two right angles, he perceives the *agreement* between the three angles of a triangle and two right angles. In the first example, the proposition is known by *intuition*: it is a disagreement "of two ideas immediately by themselves, without the intervention of any other."[4] Locke calls this degree of knowledge "the clearest and most certain that human frailty is capable of."[5] In a memorable passage, Locke characterizes intuitive knowledge as follows:

> This part of knowledge is irresistible and, like bright sunshines, forces itself immediately to be perceived, as soon as ever the mind turns its view that way; and leaves no room for hesitation, doubt, or examination, but the mind is presently filled with the clear light of it. It is on this *intuition* that depends all the certainty and evidence of all our knowledge, which certainty everyone finds to be so great that he cannot imagine, and therefore not require, a greater; for a man cannot conceive himself capable of a greater certainty than to know that any *idea* in his mind is such as he perceives it to be, and that two *ideas* wherein he perceives a difference are different and not precisely the same.[6]

In the example, the three angles of a triangle are equal to two right angles, the agreement of the ideas is perceived, not immediately, but by agreement of the ideas first with intervening ideas, and then with one another. Agreement or disagreement of ideas reached in this way is called demonstrative knowledge. In demonstration, intuition is necessary in forming the connections with intervening ideas. Locke says:

> Now, *in every step reason makes in demonstrative knowledge, there is an intuitive knowledge* of that agreement or disagreement it seeks with the next intermediate *idea* which it uses as a proof; for if it were not so, that yet would need a proof, since without the perception of such agreement or disagreement, there is no knowledge produced. If it be perceived by itself, it is intuitive knowledge; if it cannot be perceived by itself, there is need of some intervening idea, as a common measure to show their agreement or disagreement.[7]

To summarize: Our ideas are not innately stamped on our minds, but originate in experience. Once they have entered the mind, knowledge comes whenever agreement or disagreement of ideas is perceived by the mind. Such knowledge is of two degrees: (1) Intuitive knowledge, and (2) Demonstrative knowledge. Knowledge in both 1 and 2 is certain and necessary. Knowledge in 1 is self-evident and intuitive; knowledge in 2 is not self-evident, but the agreement or disagreement reached in each step of the demonstration is intuitive. Locke sometimes calls 1 and 2 *scientifical* knowledge,[8] as if to mean that fulfilling the requirements for genuine knowledge constitutes the requirements for a science.

We can now understand that Locke's empiricism was restricted to the notion that our ideas *originate* in experience, rather than being innately there from the mind's beginning. His empiricism did not stand in the way of affirming the existence of self-evident knowledge, and of holding that genuine reason consists in those activities of the mind which seek demonstrative knowledge. Morton White puts it well: "An empiricism according to which no ideas and no principles are inscribed from birth on the mind, was empiricism enough for him."[9]

To Locke's mind, mathematics was the science which most obviously had achieved demonstrative knowledge. While ethics had not yet realized its promise, Locke wrote of morality as a science capable of demonstration:

> The *idea* of a supreme Being, infinite in power, goodness, and wisdom, whose workmanship we are and on whom we depend, and the *idea* of ourselves as understanding rational beings, being such as are clear in us, would, I suppose, if duly considered and pursued, afford such foundations of our duty and rules of action as might place *morality amongst the sciences capable of demonstration:* wherein I doubt not but from self-evident propositions, by necessary consequences as incontestable as those in mathematics, the measures of right and wrong might be made out to anyone that will apply himself with the same indifferency and attention to the one as he does to the other of these sciences.[10]

While admitting that the ideas on which a demonstrative science of morality would be based cannot be represented as certainly as diagrams can represent ideas in mathematics, and that moral ideas are more difficult to illustrate than the figures commonly used in mathematics, he offered *"where there is no property there is no injustice"* as "a proposition as certain as any in Euclid."[11] Locke explains: Once the ideas of property and injustice are established, then one can know this proposition to be true as certainly as one can know the proposition, a triangle has three angles equal to two right angles, to be true. *"No government allows absolute liberty"* is another proposition mentioned by Locke as capable of being as certain as any propositions in mathematics.[12] And in the *Second Treatise of Government,* Locke speaks of a state of equality, and says, "There *being nothing more evident,* than that Creatures of the same species and rank promiscuously born to all the same advantages of Nature, and the use of the same faculties, should also be equal one amongst another without Subordination or Subjection."[13]

Yet a few certain propositions do not make a science; at most they stand as examples of the sort of propositions which Locke argued would be part of a science of ethics, if one were ever worked out. Locke wrote only as if human beings are *capable* of such a science, not that one has been developed. And he never claimed that his own writings on politics, ethics, education, and religion were examples of the sciences of action.

It is important to remind ourselves that Locke's *Essay* was concerned with *understanding*, not with knowledge alone. In Locke's words:

> The understanding faculties being given to man, not barely for speculation, but also for the conduct of his life, man would be at a great loss if he had nothing to direct him but what has the certainty of true *knowledge*. For that being very short and scanty, as we have seen, he would be often utterly in the dark, and in most of the actions of his life perfectly at a stand, had he nothing to guide him in the absence of clear and certain knowledge.[14]

Certain knowledge is taken by Locke as being so limited as to suggest to his mind that God has given it to us "probably as a taste of what intellectual creatures are capable of." And, to continue, "he has afforded us only the twilight, as I may so say, of probability."[15] Where certain knowledge is not gained we may at least determine probable connections between ideas, and have *judgment,* "whereby the mind takes its ideas to agree or disagree or, which is the same, any proposition to be true or false, without perceiving a demonstrative evidence in the proofs."[16] In short, where certain knowledge is not to be had, the mind may strive for judgment.[17] This is very much like Aristotle's poliscraftsman working amidst uncertainty and opinion, and has something in it of John of Salisbury's "probable logic." Let us again quote Locke's own words:

As demonstration is the showing the agreement or disagreement of two *ideas* by the intervention of one or more proofs which have a constant, immutable, and visible connexion one with another, so *probability* is nothing but the appearance of such an agreement or disagreement by the intervention of proofs whose connexion is not constant and immutable, or at least is not perceived to be so, but is or appears for the most part to be so, and is enough to induce the mind to *judge* the proposition to be true or false, rather than the contrary.[18]

Locke expresses a sense of the rationality of the world, a faith that men's minds are capable of understanding the nature of things and their own actions among and as a part of those very things, whether they achieve certain knowledge or judgment. He thereby takes his place in a long tradition of rationalism. Yet, as in Aristotle and John of Salisbury, Locke's is a rationalism tempered by the existence of a world that seems to resist reason, even while human beings hunger to understand that world and their actions in it. It is a rationalism mindful of the truth that the experience we have is most often something less than demonstrable; for that which is less than demonstrable we must make do with belief, with opinion; we must settle for judgments rather than knowledge. In this way, what we *understand* is a larger universe than the one we *know*; indeed, our very passion for rationality requires that we learn to live with this limitation.

Next we shall turn to the question, "What sort of writings are Locke's works that deal with subject matters of action and, in particular, with those writings that treat education most explicitly?" In dealing with this question, the relation of Locke's *Essay* to his writings on action will be at the center of our attention. To our knowledge, Locke did not call education a science; yet if he had done so, education would come under the division of the sciences which he characterized as "the skill of right applying our own powers and actions, for the attainment of things good and useful. The most considerable under this head is *ethics*, which is seeking out those rules and measures of human actions which lead to happiness, and the means to practice them."[19] This is the science of action, whose end is conduct.

The idea that in *Some Thoughts Concerning Education,* Locke's best-known work on education, he "applied his philosophy specifically to pedagogy,"[20] is found in the literature on Locke's educational thought. If "applying philosophy specifically to pedagogy" means that Locke took certain ideas from his *Essay* and tried to work out demonstrative knowledge about education; or that he attempted to take education as one of the sciences of action and establish particular educational ideas as certain and from them attempted to deduce other certain ideas; then one will not find either of these kinds of "application" in his *Education.*

John W. Yolton writes, "We must take care ... to avoid saying that, since Locke held to such and such views in the *Essay* or *Two Treatises*, his meaning in some troublesome passage in the *Education* must be such and such."[21] Yolton, in turn, quotes Nina Reicyn, who had written that it is a mistake to view Locke's *Education* as "a 'systematic enterprise designed to deduce from the philosophy of the *Essay* the educational applications which it entails.' "[22] Yolton goes so far as to contend: "Even to draw piecemeal connections between the two works is dangerous."[23] Yolton and Reicyn are most instructive in their insistence that it is difficult to find "connections" between Locke's *Essay* and his *Some Thoughts Concerning Education,* by finding intuitive or demonstrative knowledge in the former and using it as a basis from which certain propositions are deduced in the latter. If Locke had sought such connections, he might have taken from the *Essay* the idea that the mind is a *tabula rasa* and, together with other ideas, he might have deduced certain propositions on education as examples of demonstrative knowledge. Yet he does not do this. If there is any system to be found by taking Locke's writings as a whole, Yolton thinks, it "tends to emerge out of, rather than control, what Locke writes."[24]

There is another way of finding a relationship between the *Essay* and the *Education* which enables us to put aside the above-mentioned sense in which the *Education* would be an "applied" *Essay*. This other kind of relationship is suggested by Locke's own distinction between knowledge and judgment. We find no knowledge-claim in the *Education* that meets the criterion either of intuitive knowledge or of demonstrative knowledge. Instead, we find judgment. If "applying" his philosophy to pedagogy is taken to mean that Locke's mind is at work *judging* propositions to agree rather than at work *knowing* their constant and immutable connections, then in his own terms we have probability instead of certainty, judgment instead of knowledge.

To put it differently, we do not find explicit applications or connections relating any claims about intuitive or demonstrative knowledge to his writings on action. Instead, we find the kind of relation which stands forth when Locke's mind deals with subject matters that yield judgments rather than knowledge. This is so because the agreements and disagreements between the propositions which Locke determines in his *Education* and other writings on conduct are probable rather than certain. The point emphasized here is a simple one: The fact that Locke did not write a demonstrative science of education, or make explicit connections between his *Essay* and his writings on action, should not be surprising, inasmuch as he shows us in his *Essay* that the realm of understanding is larger than that of knowledge, and that the subject matters of action may be understood in some way, even if they cannot be known. They may be understood as judgment.

Indeed, there is a passage quoted by Laslett from Locke's journal in which he casts doubt upon his own idea that ethics is capable of demonstration:

> The well management of public or private affairs depending upon the various and unknown humours, interests and capacities of men we have to do with in the world, and not upon any settled ideas of things physical, polity and prudence are not capable of demonstration. But a man is principally helped in them by the history of matter of fact, and a sagacity of finding out an analogy in their operations and effects.[25]

This sagacity is just the kind of wisdom possessed by one whose experience shows him that probability and judgment, lacking the certainty and immediate satisfaction which come with true knowledge, are the best that we can determine in particular contexts of action. One mark of such "common sense wisdom" is the willingness to continue to develop understanding, even though it is of a kind that falls short of true knowledge. And if Locke's own writings on action be viewed in this light, they will show us that the "natural histories of fact," or of action, will not yield to the demands of certainty. The natural histories of action, if one is true to the uncertain and probable nature of the ideas they bring to mind, simply cannot be forced to conform to the demands of strict demonstration. Locke's practice of building natural histories in subject matters of action shows us that Locke did not allow his passion for certainty and demonstration to overcome his passion for a larger but less certain understanding.

In contrasting Locke's political writings with those of Hobbes, Laslett characterizes Hobbes as presenting synthetic systems, "a view of the world which proceeded from an account of reality to an account of knowledge, and so to an ethic and to politics."[26] He suggests that if there was not a Lockeian philosophy in that sense, there was a "Lockeian attitude," which he characterizes in the context of "natural law" in Locke's writings:

> Natural law was, in this analysis, a part of his rationalism, his conviction that the universe is to be understood rationally, even the workings of the deity, even the relations of human beings, but at all points it must be compared with, made to fit into, the observed, the empirical facts about the created world and human behaviour.[27]

Locke does not discuss a "natural law" to be followed in his educational writings, but he does write about that which is "natural" to human beings,[28] and works at understanding how human beings may learn to do things that are natural to them. In a rational world, for example, it would be natural for people to behave toward others without affectation. But the demands of others behaving in nonrational ways, together with the accidents of circumstance, make it difficult to act in natural ways. Hence the *Education* may be taken as a "natural history" of facts and opinions about education, a study in judgment, in which some understanding is gained, even though it may not be all that one seeking certainty and demonstration would desire. Whether or not ethical and educational laws can be discovered, Locke's writings are examples of the attitude that some rationality is possible in human affairs, and the sort of understanding which judgment provides is a better guide than no understanding at all.

"Virtue is harder to get than a knowledge of the world,"[29] Locke writes, and puts virtue "as the first and most necessary of those endowments that belong to a man or a gentleman."[30] As in Aristotle and the oratorical tradition, the aim is to accustom children to the truths in commonplaces, and to submit them to reason before they are capable of fully understanding what Truth is, or of reasoning after the manner of one who possesses Wisdom. The kind of understanding which judgment brings, a Lockeian counterpart of Aristotle's prudence and of Cicero's attention to commonplaces, is apparent when Locke writes:

> The rest [of that which is required to prepare a child for wisdom] which is to be learned from time, experience, and observation, and an acquaintance with men, their tempers and designs, is not to be expected in the ignorance and inadvertancy of childhood.[31]

True, Locke says that we should reason with children, but by this he does not mean that they should be treated as little philosophers. Instead, "it must be by such reasons as their age and understanding are capable of."[32] They are not capable of "reasonings from remote principles," Locke argues, adding, "the reasons that move them must be obvious, and level to their thoughts, and such as may ... be felt and touched."[33] While it is doubtful that Locke thought of the integrity of childlike reasoning as Rousseau was to do when he wrote of a "mature child," it is clear that Locke was extremely sensitive to the importance of reasoning with children in ways that respect their ways of being. Locke did not write enough about "childhood reasoning" to enable us to construct a detailed account of a Lockeian conception of child development. At the same time, what stands out is the sense in which a certain "attitude" or way of conducting ourselves in reasoning with children, accompanied by our attempts to find direct and simple connections between ideas, is essential to their growth.

The large place which activity has in understanding, and the sense that knowing and judging are modes of action, ways of conducting ourselves, has been suggested above. In a striking way, Locke accentuates the importance of conduct in understanding in the title he gave to one work, *Of the Conduct of the Understanding*. The idea suggested by this title is not merely that conduct is important for understanding, but that understanding itself is a way of conducting ourselves. Locke puts it in this way: "Great care should be taken of the understanding *to conduct it right* in the search of knowledge and of the judgments it makes."[34] As in his *Thoughts on Education*, so in his *Conduct,* he argues that it is practice that makes the mind what it is,[35] that "while natural disposition may often give the first rise to it ... it is practice alone that brings the powers of the mind as well as those of the body to their perfection."[36] Locke's "environmentalism," his prospects for education, perhaps are even stronger than in the eye of his classical predecessors like Isocrates and Quintilian, who also held practice in high regard. Locke says, "the differences so observable in men's understandings and parts does not arise so much from their natural faculties as acquired habits."[37] The point to be made here, again, is that, while Locke does not apply certain propositions from his *Essay* directly to matters of education, his keen sense is that our knowing and judging are matters of experience rather than of innate possession. This leads him to engage in judging by conducting his own understanding in educational contexts. In all matters, whether they be the origins of our knowlege, or in understanding subject matters of action, the aim is to learn how to conduct ourselves with the prospect that, in so doing, we may continue to improve our conduct.

One category in Locke's consideration of understanding is distinct from either knowledge or judgment, both of which are determined by reason. This is the category of faith, which Locke calls "the assent to any proposition, not ... made out by the deductions of reason, but upon the credit of the proposer as coming from God, in some extra-ordinary ways of communication."[38] This way of discovering truths is called revelation. Yet the truths we determine by the intuitions of our minds are more certain than those shown us by revelation. "The knowledge we have that this *revelation* came at first from God can never be so sure as the knowledge we have from the clear and distinct perception of the agreement or disagreement of our own ideas."[39] Further, assent cannot be given to any proposition which is contradictory to our intuitive knowledge, whether immediately as in self-evident propositions, or by deductions of reason that are gained in demonstrative knowledge. Thus, if propositions are contrary to the perception of the agreement or disagreement of our ideas, they cannot be urged as matters of faith. Many things, however, are "beyond the discovery of our natural faculties and above *reason*."[40] These things, when revealed, are the "proper matter of faith." As an example, the proposition, "the dead shall rise again," is "beyond the discovery of reason," purely a matter of faith.[41] Even in these matters, whose truths reason has no part in determining, "it still belongs to *reason* to judge of the truth of its being a revelation and of the significance of the words wherein it is delivered."[42] Locke admits another sort of proposition requiring our assent as a matter of faith: a probable proposition in which reason has not determined its certain truth or falsity and where a clear and evident revelation does so. "*Reason*, in that particular matter, being able to reach no higher than probability, *faith* gave the determination where *reason* came short, and *revelation* discovered on which side the truth lay."[43]

We have seen that Locke had held forth the possibility of a demonstrative science of morality in his *Essay*. In his notes, he had questioned this possibility, likening the study which reason brings to ethics to a natural history of facts and opinions in such a way that reason arrives at judgment rather than knowlege. In his *Reasonableness of Christianity* Locke maintains that revelation has entered into history to provide truths useful to Christian philosophers in establishing morality "upon its true foundation."[44] According to Locke, it is a matter of historical record that "natural religion in its full extent, was no where, that I know, taken care of, by the force of natural reason."[45] The truths added by Christian philosophers to those of philosophers before the Saviour's time, "is owing to revelation: though as soon as they are heard and considered, they are found to be agreeable to reason; and such as by no means can be contradicted."[46]

Thus the moral precepts necessary for our conduct are not determined by reason alone; they have been revealed to us and are put past doubt by the evidence set forth in the Scriptures; e.g., miracles performed by Jesus Christ show that he was sent by God. This evidence is not contradictory to reason, but is agreeable to reason: in such a way reason is joined to revelation to provide moral precepts that reason, working by itself, has been unable to determine. Indeed, Locke goes so far as to maintain that the precepts of Jesus Christ as witnessed in the Scriptures constitute "a full and sufficient rule for our direction."[47] He provides an example of such a precept: "Our Saviour's great rule, that we should love our neighbor as ourselves is such a fundamental truth for regulating human society, that, I think, by that alone one might without difficulty determine all the cases and doubts in social morality."[48]

In one sense, such principles constitute a more nearly adequate basis for a "science of action" than the one suggested by the few "self-evident principles" Locke mentions in the *Essay* and *Second Treatise*. If we add to these his *Education* as a science of action, we find precious few statements that stand as certain "principles of conduct." Put differently, of the subject matters which bear upon the sciences of action, only the one whose precepts are revealed, not found by reason, constitutes "a full and sufficient rule for our direction." The others, in particular, politics and education, do not enjoy the sort of clarity which revelation provides and reason cannot deny: students of these labor with probability instead of certainty; their study yields judgment instead of knowledge.

Yet, even in *Reasonableness of Christianity,* Locke does not write a science of action. Instead, he maintains that the moral precepts found in the Scriptures stand as a rule for our direction. If they do not make up a science of action, at least a body of precepts exists in the Scriptures: these are reasonable, i.e., they constitute evidence which our minds are capable of taking which put us past doubt. It is almost as if we do not need a science of action in the moral realm determined by reason, at least insofar as the precepts of the Scriptures are capable of guiding us. Now, if Locke had been a systematic philosopher, we might expect him to have taken those moral precepts as principles of a science of action and to have attempted to demonstrate other propositions bearing upon action. Yet even here Locke runs true to the form that we have discussed earlier. One is tempted to say that the Scriptures provide a kind of evidence for Locke. They are one kind of "natural history" which brings moral precepts to our attention. Again, Locke's common sense restrains him from insisting upon more than the *evidence* provided by the Scriptures. His *empiricism* expressed earlier as an *attitude* restrains his rationalism.

Locke's ideas have endured to influence educational thinking from the eighteenth century to the present. Among the writings which claim Locke in their genealogy, those which emphasize sensations in the origins of knowing, and those which made out of sensationalism a strong environmentalism, are probably best known to students of educational theory. Yet the point we press is that his writings show us a *rationalistic* tradition which developed alongside the *sensationalistic* one. In the rationalistic tradition, conduct is prized as much as in any tradition of sensationalism. Isaac Watts (1676–1748) takes his place in this tradition of Lockeian rationalism. Watts, like Locke, did not try to deduce propositions about education from rationalistic principles. In his own way, Watts foreshadows John Dewey in the way he treats logic as a method of inquiry.

The subtitle of Watts' *Logic* is *The Right Use of Reason in the Enquiry after Truth,* suggesting that his logic has in common with Locke's *Essay* a concern for a universe of understanding larger than that under the control of formal rules of logic. Watts supplemented his *Logic* with *The Improvement of the Mind,* a work on self-education and the education of others; another work, the *Discourse on the Education of Children and Youth,* serves the same end. In one sense, the "right use of reason in the inquiry after truth" is itself a way of getting an education. If that sense is acknowledged, Watts' *Logic,* together with its supplements, constitutes a rather thoroughgoing treatise on educational theory. In their own way, Watts' writings on logic constitute his "conduct of the understanding." This means that Watts' *Logic,* as a study of the art of inquiry, is inescapably a kind of educational theory, insofar as logic is a practical art combining right knowledge and action. At the same time, his logic is a conception of conduct.

Watts defines logic as "the art of using reason well in our enquiries after truth, and the communication of it to others."[49] The right use and improvement of our intellectual powers are necessary, not only to attain knowledge, but to govern the actions of life. "It is the cultivation of our reason by which we are better enabled to distinguish good from evil, as well as truth from falsehood."[50] As an art, logic takes for its province both the use of reason whose aim is to attain knowledge and the use of reason to improve human conduct; like Locke's *Essay,* Watts' *Logic* provides an illustration of the argument that reasoning calls for certain kinds of action. Essentially, Watts considers logic as conduct in two senses: (1) reasoning itself is a kind of activity, a way of conducting oneself; and (2) the outcomes gained through reason to realize other ends constitute another kind of activity.

What Watts calls the principal operations of the mind show us the ways in which logic is an activity of both mind and conduct. One operation of the mind Watts calls "perception," which is "the mere simple contemplation of things offered to the mind, without affirming or denying anything about them."[51] Another operation is "judgment," the joining of two or more ideas to form sentences known as propositions. A third, "argumentation," is the construction of syllogisms so as to constitute arguments. In Watts' characterization of the fourth operation of the mind, "disposition," we find the idea that reasoning itself is a way of conducting life. Disposition is the organization of ideas, propositions, and arguments (which Watts calls the "effects" of the other three operations) in such a way as "to gain the clearest knowledge of it, to retain it longest, and to explain it to others in the best manner."[52] Watts says that the effect of the operation called disposition is *method.* Organizing and explaining things in a certain manner is a way of doing things. This means that disposition should not be conceived as operating apart from conduct; rather, it is a disposition to organize materials so that certain ways of conducting ourselves will come to pass.

Watts discusses two senses of method: "the largest sense," and "a more limited sense."[53] (1) In the former, the interest in conduct is apparent: "Method ... implies the placing of several things, or performing several operations in such an order as is most convenient to attain some end proposed."[54] Quite clearly, such an end may be an end of conduct, and the conduct of oneself and others in gaining an education might well be taken as an example of this sort of method. (2) In a more limited sense, which Watts says is the way method is usually taken in the study of logic, "Method is the disposition of a variety of thoughts on any subject in such order as may best serve to find out unknown truths, to explain and confirm truths that are known, or to fix them in the memory."[55] Here method is made possible by the outcomes of perception, judgment, and argumentation in the subject matter under investigation, and is accompanied by a tendency to do something with the outcomes, to conduct oneself in certain ways in their use.

In discussing "disposition," which is a part of the art of logic, we return to the beginning of Watts' *Logic.* There he has emphasized the right use of reason in serving two ends: attaining knowledge, and governing the actions of life. For Watts, distinguishing truth from falsehood and good from evil are affairs of reason; learning how to *act* in accord with good rather than in accord with evil is also an affair of reason. In sum, Watts' *Logic* is a kind of enquiry after truth which we may call action, or conduct. Watts calls it an art, rather than a science; the basis for this distinction is that "art" refers chiefly to practice, "science" to speculation.[56] Yet both art and science, practice and speculation, are ways of conduct.

Like Locke before him, Watts distinguished between two degrees of knowledge. Watts' "certain propositions," "where the evidence of the agreement or disagreement of the ideas is so strong and plain, that we cannot forbid or delay our assent,"[57] brings to mind Locke's genuine knowledge. And Watts' "doubtful or uncertain" propositions, "when there is an obscurity upon the agreement or disagreement of the ideas, so that the mind does not clearly perceive it, and is not compelled to assent or dissent,"[58] is the counterpart of Locke's judgment. Certain propositions constitute knowledge; uncertain ones constitute judgment.

Watts' writings on conduct were based on a thoroughgoing rationalism, affirming the imperative that the knowledge and opinion one gets can be gained only through one's own activities. Again, the most fundamental and precious activity is the right use of reason. As in Locke, "even the matters of revelation are to be believed by us, because our reason pronounces the revelation to be true. God ... cannot ... require us to assent to anything without reasonable or sufficient evidence, nor to believe any proposition more strongly than what our evidence for it will support."[59] This means that in matters of religion, as in other matters, we may have both knowledge and opinion. What Watts calls the "government of self" takes on a particular meaning when the emphasis is placed upon education, a meaning which illustrates his concern to understand logic as an art of inquiry involving conduct. Watts holds that we become educated if we learn to adapt methods in ways such that they become a fundamental part of our very conduct.

Watts, again like Locke, did not write a *system* in the sense that he might have taken certain propositions gained in his *Right Use of Reason in the Enquiry after Truth* and attempted to deduce other propositions from them by "natural methods." At one point he does say that a principle of morality, "Do that to others which you think just and reasonable that others should do to you," is likened to the doctrine of gravitation in natural philosophy as a fundamental truth.[60] Yet this fundamental principle of morality was not treated as an axiom of a demonstrative science of conduct, but as a directive principle by which one may set some practical limits to the ends and means in conduct. Such a directive principle does not promise certainty, let alone guarantee that things done will be just and reasonable; rather it may enable us to *aim* for just and reasonable conduct by rationally chosen means.

The following appears to be the most succinct statement of the general principle which Watts believed is best to follow in the government of self: "In matters of practice we should be most careful to fix our end right and wisely determine the scope at which we aim, because that is to direct us in the choice and use of all the means to attain it."[61] The art of conducting inquiry into the improvement of the mind is a way of finding how to conduct oneself according to the nature of the practice he is trying to improve; it is through a kind of conduct in which one *applies himself* rather than an application of principles of knowledge to a particular subject matter. What is natural and rational about conduct are the ways in which it resists being shaped according to demonstrable principles of knowledge. "There are many things even in religion," Watts maintains, "as well as in philosophy and the civil life, which we believe with very different degrees of assent, and this is or should be always regulated according to the different degrees of evidence which we enjoy."[62]

One example of Watts' conception of conduct, a manifestation of his idea of "government of self" discussed in the context of educating children, is expressed in this passage:

> Tell them that they must not judge of things by custom, nor by the common opinions of the multitude, nor by the practices of the rich and the great: For all these things may deceive them: but that they must judge of things merely by reasoning, except in matters of religion, and there they must judge rather by scripture, or the word of God.[63]

Children begin to learn the art of conducting themselves in natural, human, and divine subject matters. This art is made possible by the knowledge and opinions human beings already possess. At the same time one who possesses the art will recognize that it will remain but a possibility for the young until they learn the art of conduct for themselves. Thus Watts' rationalism and his strong sense of the necessity of self-government are joined in his insistence that the universe of things natural, human, and divine must function as a part *of* human conduct in the extent to which the universe known by God is man's province as well. In that sense, conduct which is self-government aims to be rational. And logic, as the art of inquiry, is at best a limited means to the end of realizing such conduct.

The rationalistic tradition to which Locke and Watts belong has held forth the possibility that human conduct might be bettered if human beings try to understand what reason would show them is natural and good. Yet it is not enough to understand in some merely *mental* way. For Locke and Watts, understanding in one sense already is a kind of conduct. In another sense, understanding requires changes in conduct if reason and revelation are to be taken seriously in the educational affairs of human beings.

and the study method which reveals the uncertain and probable character of human experience is the most difficult to undertake but the most important to possess.

Like Aristotle, Vico found study of the conduct of life to be less precise than mathematics and physics, but no less important. He argued that "it is an error to apply to the prudent conduct of life the abstract criterion of reasoning that obtains in the domain of science."[1] "Young people are to be educated in common sense,"[2] Vico insists, and criticized those Cartesians of his day who had young students first take up philosophical criticism. "Young minds are too immature, too unsure to derive benefits from it,"[3] he goes on. If their common sense is strengthened, "they can grow in prudence and eloquence."[4] After they have acquired common sense, they may then study philosophical criticism.[5] The best instrument for acquiring common sense is the art of topics, by which we invent arguments. Vico sums it up neatly: "Since the invention of arguments is by nature prior to the judgment of their validity . . . in teaching . . . invention should be given priority over philosophical criticism."[6]

A student should take care to become skilled in *topics*, the art of finding "middle terms," i.e., the likely or probable explanation that comes from studying both sides of a question. "Let him not spurn reasons that wear a semblance of probability and verisimilitude,"[7] says Vico. In the affairs of conduct that constitute social life, it is common sense that is needed more than the precision of the geometric method and the principles determined by the science of physics. Literally, the *sense* of the matter to which one is subjected in studies of conduct is that which is *common*. As Vico puts it, "Common sense arises from perceptions based on verisimilitude. Probabilities stand, so to speak, midway between truth and falsity, since things which most of the time are true, are only very seldom false."[8]

Vico uses the example of Cicero, "who asserts that his own eloquence is chiefly due to the art of skillfully arranging a set of effective lines of argument,"[9] against the Cartesians who wanted to put the geometric method of philosophical criticism at the service of conduct. The skillful orator, unlike the physicist who proceeds "by placing primary axioms first," Vico writes, "omits things that are well known, and while impressing on his hearers secondary truth, he tacitly reminds them of the primal points he has left out and while he carries through his argument, his listeners are made to feel that they are completing it themselves."[10] Vico's art of inventing arguments, including practice in finding probable explanations, is his way of bringing alive and articulating the sense that is common to orator and listeners; as in Cicero's commonplaces, it is as if the common sense so important to Vico has to grow out of and be expressed through experience lived by orator and listeners. In holding that human nature "is difficult to determine" and that "the art of seemly conduct in life" is "the most difficult of all arts",[11] Vico argues that too much attention is paid to the natural sciences and not enough to ethics and politics.[12] Furthermore, those who apply the methods of science in judging human actions are "doctrinaires," Vico holds. "Satisfied with abstract truth alone, and not being gifted with common sense, unused to follow probability, those doctrinaires do not bother to find out whether their opinion is held by the generality and whether the things that are truths to them are also such to other people."[13] The study of both poetry and philosophy adds a needed dimension to the study of topics, and complements by example of action and character the possibilities of human conduct. He finds poets to be "no less eager in the pursuit of truth than philosophers";[14] both treat moral duties; both depict human behavior in action. "The poet teaches by delighting what the philosopher teaches austerely,"[15] Vico says. Yet the poet's examples of action and character are invented; in doing this, the poet departs from daily semblances of truth, with which the moral philosopher must deal. To put it differently, the moral philosopher, one experienced in the common sense of action and the probable character of judgments about human conduct, is confined to the world of unpredictable, uncertain human behavior. Yet the poet sets forth "a more constant, more abiding reality," a reality that, in a sense, is "more real than physical reality itself."[16] Later, in the *New Science*, Vico the investigator is to be something of poet-and-philosopher, emphasizing a union of the two rather than a separation of them; there the imagination of the poet and the reason of the philosopher are so joined that they are really difficult to distinguish in the midst of the subject matter. In the *Study Methods*, Vico had put the distinction as follows: "Practical judgment in human affairs seeks out the truth as it is, although truth may be deeply hidden under imprudence, ignorance, whim, fatality, or chance; whereas poetry focuses her gaze on truth as it ought to be by nature and reason."[17] It should be clear now, that when writing his *Study Methods*, Vico stood essentially in the tradition of those, like Aristotle, who respect the integrity of the various subject matters and believe that the development of human integrity is contingent upon protecting matters of conduct from intrusions by the geometric method. To argue that the study of politics needs to be treated in terms of a methodology appropriate to it which differs from the methodologies of geometry or of physics is a kind of Aristotelian respect for the idea of distinct sciences.

Even so, Vico had not yet made the discovery which was to be the key to his *New Science*. After reading Bacon's *Novum Organon* which had shown him "how the sciences as they now stand may be perfected," Vico was to write his own "Novum Organon" of history, which disclosed "the ancient world of the sciences, how crude they were in their origins, and how they were gradually refined until they reached the form in which we have received them."[18] Before Vico was able to create a new science, he had to learn to put to use an idea that he had already held in the *Study Methods*. There he had argued that subject matters of conduct are not susceptible to the geometrical method; he had argued also that physics is not susceptible to the geometrical method. In doing so, the essential principle of his conception of knowledge was set forth, a principle that was to be put to different use in the *New Science*. In the *Study Methods* he said:

> The principles of physics which are put forward as truths on the strength of the geometrical method are not really truths, but wear a semblance of probability. The method by which they were reached is that of geometry, but physical truths so elicited are not demonstrated as reliably as are geometrical axioms. We are able to demonstrate geometrical propositions because we create them; were it possible for us to supply demonstrations of propositions of physics, we would be capable of creating them *ex nihilo* as well.[19]

This criticism of what Vico took to be an overextended and misplaced application of the geometrical method came from the essential principle of his theory of knowledge, according to which only the maker or creator can know that which is made or created. Thus men can know mathematics, because they create it. Yet its objects stand as fictions, not real parts of the natural world. Because God created the world of nature, only God can perfectly know that world. Vico continued, "The archetypal *forms*, the ideal patterns of reality, exist in God alone. The physical nature of things, the phenomenal world, is modeled after those archetypes."[20] We can know physics insofar as we are able to experiment. In a sense, we *make* experiments which show us something of the world of nature that has been created by God; yet not having created the objects which our experiments bring to mind, we can not know those objects as their creator can.

What Vico came to believe, what enabled him to write the *New Science*, was the idea that the early founders of society were not "rational" like Plato, Aristotle, Descartes, and Vico himself. Vico had come to believe, instead, that they were beastlike creatures who did not possess language, law, or institutions. He had come to extend his idea, already expressed in the *Study Methods*, that the maker or creator can know what he has made or created, to the world of human conduct. That is, human conduct no longer is merely what is to be studied by the method of the *ars topica*, complemented by a sense of philosophy seeking probabilities in the midst of an uncertain world and by poetry which invents a more certain reality, as if the reality is just what it is, fixed once and for all time. Rather the reality has been made by human beings, celebrated in their poetry, and discussed in their *ars topica* and in their philosophy. It might be better said that their poetic and rational activities were in and of the making, not just celebrations of and discussions about a reality already made. A way of understanding the reality is to view it as *understandable* for a reason that Vico either did not see or did not acknowledge when he wrote the *Study Methods*: just because human beings have made themselves as social beings, they can know their nature. Thus the study of human conduct, entitled to its own method but not honored as a *science* in the *Study Methods*, is now a science. It is Vico's *New Science*.

The early peoples were poets, not philosophers, and spoke in poetic characters, not in reasoned discourse. As Vico put it:

> This discovery, which is the master key of this Science, has cost us the persistent research of almost all of our literary life, because with our civilized natures we [moderns] cannot at all imagine and can understand only by great toil the poetic nature of these first men. The [poetic] characters of which we speak were certain imaginative genera (images for the most part of animated substances, of gods or heroes, formed by their imagination) to which they reduced all the species or all the particulars appertaining to each genus.[21]

Human beings can know the "world of civil society," the subject matters constituting their lives and their institutions, because in their history human beings have made that world. The key to understanding this world is celebrated by Vico in this passage:

> But in the night of thick darkness enveloping the earliest antiquity, so remote from ourselves, there shines the eternal and never failing light of a truth beyond all question: that the world of civil society has certainly been made by men, and that its principles are therefore to be found within the modifications of our own human mind. Whoever reflects on this cannot but marvel that the philosophers should have bent all their energies to the study of the world of nature, which, since God made it, He alone knows; and that they should have neglected the study of the world of nations, or civil world, which, since men had made it, men could come to know.[22]

In his *New Science* Vico provides an account of the origins of poetry and philosophy which enables us to understand the sense in which the origins were ways of conduct as well as ways of imagining and understanding the conduct itself. Vico tries to find out how we may let each of them, poetry and philosophy, have its way with us, and how we may learn to take each on its own terms. The social nature of poetry and philosophy is emphasized in Vico's account in their striving to express what is common to the sense of human beings in their relations with one another. Vico's account of the nature of institutions and Aristotle's account of the nature of the city-state are similar. Vico writes, "The nature of institutions is nothing but their coming into being at certain times and in certain guises."[23] Further, his notion of the importance of the origins of things is set forth in this axiom: "Doctines must take their beginning from that of the matters of which they treat."[24] Here are joined his earlier interest in determining the integrity of each subject matter by finding out how to take it on its own terms with his discovery that the nature of the new science can be determined by studying the genesis of institutions which men themselves have made through a long history. We have pointed to Aristotle's similar concern "to expect that amount of exactness in each kind which the nature of the particular subject admits." It remains to point to Aristotle's claim that "the best method of investigation is to study things in the process of development from the beginning."

Vico, like Aristotle, begins where the subject matter begins. And, like Aristotle, he follows the subject matter to the ends where it naturally leads. But where Vico adds a new dimension of meaning to *origins*, and to *ends*, is in his discovery that in the study of the new science the investigator must try to sense

> how the founders of gentile humanity by means of their natural theology (or metaphysics) imagined the gods; how by means of their logic they invented languages; by morals, created heroes; by economics, founded families, and by politics, cities; by their physics, established the beginnings of things as all divine; by the particular physics of man, in a certain sense created themselves.[25]

This means that the nature of poetry, philosophy, and the arts has come into being, has been made by the activities of human beings as they have created themselves. Further, it means that there is no one nature to be grasped by human reason and applied to all subject matters. To gain some sense of the natures of the arts and the institutions that have been created, the investigator must use his imagination and attempt to know what human beings were like in their beginnings and follow these beginnings to their natural ends which are found in the presence of the investigator.

Certain natural tendencies of the human being get in the way of investigators. These tendencies are a prospect for understanding and at the same time, an obstacle in the way of understanding. Vico's suggestion, "because of the indefinite nature of the human mind, wherever it is lost in ignorance man makes himself the measure of all things,"[26] is one example. It points to a way of beginning Vico's account of the poetry making tendency by which civil society had its beginnings; it also points to the error of rational men in supposing that rationality is the measure of things. Another example is Vico's notion that "it is another property of the human mind that whenever men can form no idea of distant and unknown things, they judge them by what is familiar and at hand."[27] The early human beings, with their large imaginations, wrote fables in which particulars were enlarged:

> On this there is a fine passage in Aristotle in which he remarks that men of limited ideas erect every particular into a maxim. The reason must be that the human mind, which is indefinite, being constricted by the vigor of the senses, cannot otherwise express its almost divine nature than by thus enlarging particulars in imagination. It is perhaps on this account that in both the Greek and the Latin poets the images of gods and heroes always appear larger than those of men.[28]

We must notice also that the methodological difficulty of all rationalists, the difficulty which Vico himself worked through, is that of judging subject matters and institutions as though they were created largely by the rationality of human beings. Vico thought that the first men were "stupid, insensate, and horrible beasts," wondered at things, and gave them substance after their own ideas, "just as children do, whom we see take inanimate things in their hands and play with them and talk to them as though they were living persons."[29] The powerful imaginations of the first men created the beginnings of a poetry by which they could measure the things for which the poetry stood. In a sense, they created a metaphysics, an account of the way things are, which was also a logic, "insofar as it considers things in all the forms by which they may be signified."[30] Through the poetry which they created, the first men gave expression to a kind of wisdom, a poetic wisdom.

> Hence poetic wisdom, the first wisdom of the gentile world, must have begun with a metaphysics not rational and abstract like that of learned men now, but felt and imagined as that of these first men must have been, who, without power of ratiocination, were all robust sense and vigorous imagination. This metaphysics was their poetry, a faculty born with them (for they were furnished by nature with these senses and imaginations); born of their ignorance of causes, for ignorance, the mother of wonder, made everything wonderful to men who were ignorant of everything.[31]

The first men created things according to their own ideas, and by creating them, came to believe in them. The proper material of poetry, in its origins, Vico calls "the credible impossibility."[32] Vico maintains that the first poets, giving names to things from the most particular and most sensible ideas, were different from the philosophers, such as Plato and Aristotle, whose minds sought the most universal ideas as principles of explanation. Vico summarizes his work on the relation between poetic, or vulgar wisdom, and philosophic, or esoteric wisdom, as follows:

> Throughout this book, it will be shown that as much as the poets had first sensed in the way of vulgar wisdom, the philosophers later understood in the way of esoteric wisdom; so that the former may be said to have been the sense and the latter the intellect of the human race. What Aristotle said of the individual man is therefore true of the race in general: *Nihil est in intellectu quin prius fuerit in sensu.* That is, the human mind does not understand anything of which it has had no previous impression (which our modern metaphysicians call 'occasion') from the senses. Now the mind uses the intellect when, from something it senses, it gathers something which does not fall under the senses; and this is the proper meaning of the Latin verb *intelligere.*[33]

Poetic metaphysics is unable to understand things in a way in which a later, rational metaphysics understands them. Each is a way of doing things, a way by which human beings conduct themselves in "sensing" and "intellecting." Now to try to understand the poetic metaphysics according to the terms of a rationalistic metaphysics is to do violence to the former and to ask the latter to do something for which it is not suited. Vico argues that in all languages the greater part of expressions referring to inanimate things takes shape as metaphors, from parts of the human body and from human senses and passions, e.g., head for top or beginning, foot for end or bottom, heart for center. Then he says:

> Man in his ignorance makes himself the rule of the universe, for in the examples cited he has made of himself an entire world. So that, as rational metaphysics teaches that man becomes all things by understanding them, this imaginative metaphysics shows that man becomes all things by *not* understanding them; and perhaps the latter proposition is truer than the former, for when man understands he extends his mind and takes in the things, but when he does not understand he makes the things out of himself and becomes them by transforming himself into them.[34]

Making things out of oneself, becoming them, and transforming oneself into them, may now be taken as a disposition to sense things by acting to *become* these things. The poetic metaphysics of Vico is imagination's work, taken as a kind of hungering to make the world in one's own image. In a sense, one strives to be the world that one is making. Eventually, however, the hungering becomes a rational metaphysics, a desire to take the world on its own terms, to understand it. Yet, in rational metaphysics, something of the earlier hungering remains. The difficulty in taking the world on its own terms is due to the tendency of the human mind to shape it according to its own fears, wishes and dispositions, to strive to become that world. Let us recall Vico's suggestion that whenever man is lost in ignorance he tends to make himself the measure of all things; and he judges distant and unknown things by what is familiar and at hand. The efforts of rational metaphysics to understand the world are difficult be- cause the imagination of the rational metaphysician, an echo of the poetic metaphysics at work, tends to create a world of its own even while it is bringing the already-created world into the categories of the understand- ing.

In a sense, then, both poetic and rational metaphysics are striving to bring worlds into being even while they are striving to understand those worlds. Put differently, poetic metaphysics cannot help creating at the same time as rational metaphysics is trying to understand a world that is already created. One *creates* while the other *knows*; yet each is a kind of creator and each is a kind of knower. At the same time, the earlier creations of poetic metaphysics live on, in our institutions, our literature, our arts of making, doing, and thinking.

Vico characterizes the early history of human beings at work creating poetic metaphysics in this passage:

> In that human indigence, the peoples, who were almost all body and almost no reflection, must have been all vivid sensation in perceiving particulars, strong imagination in apprehending and enlarging them, sharp wit in refer- ring them to their imaginative genera, and robust memory in retaining them. It is true that these faculties appertain to the mind, but they have their roots in the body and draw their strength from it. Hence memory is the same as imagination which for that reason is called *memoria* in Latin.[35]

In this we are reminded of Aristotle's account of knowing in the *Posterior Analytics*, the account so important to John of Salisbury, where memory is taken as coming out of sense perception, experience as developing from repeated memories, and the universal taking its shape in experience. In Vico, referring sense perceptions to "imagined genera" is an activity of imagination and of memory, the two so indistinguishable in their function- ing that the same word may stand for both. Yet Vico argues that the method by which the vulgar poets expressed their wisdom is fundamentally differ- ent from the method of rational metaphysics:

> By the very nature of poetry it is impossible for anyone to be at the same time a sublime poet and a sublime metaphysician, for metaphysics abstracts the

mind from the senses, and the poetic faculty must submerge the whole mind in the senses; metaphysics soars up to universals, and the poetic faculty must plunge deep into particulars.[36]

Vico's celebration of poetic wisdom as a forerunner of philosophic wisdom, along with the idea that men have made the world of civil institutions, brings added meaning to our efforts to understand human activities as kinds of art which are ways of taking action.

In contributing to the making of society, poetic wisdom has inescapably contributed to the making of human beings. What they have become can be determined by the working of a new kind of philosophic wisdom, a new science. That new science seeks to understand the "modifications of our own human mind." What had been the domain of Aristotle's poliscraftsman now takes on the significance of being human in a particular way: considered in its history, as it comes into being through time, this domain requires a sensitivity to imagination's work which enables us to gain a different perspective on both the natural and the human studies. Vico writes, "Memory . . . has three different aspects: memory when it remembers things, imagination when it alters or imitates them, and invention when it gives them a new turn or puts them into proper arrangement and relationship."[37] Here he is packing so many meanings into one term that a discipline is called for which is at once history, poetry, philosophy, and all the other arts created by human beings. The history of human beings living in society is the development of a certain kind of imagination, memory, and philosophy; such a history is poetry no less than it is philosophy. The remark by the poet Shelley, that "the true poetry of Rome lived in its institutions," points to one side of Vico's insight that institutions embody the part of human history which philosophic wisdom tries to understand. The development of human society, along with its philosophic wisdom, brings Aristotle's poliscraftsmen into a history in which what they are doing is making themselves. In their doing and making, they are creating themselves and their society through their imagining, their remembering, their inventing, and their understanding. Aristotle's poliscraftsman had begun his investigation and his doing with an idea of "that which is to be." Vico's poetic metaphysician and rational metaphysician, each in his own way, creates an account of what he is and how he came to be. What is natural and necessary in the account of both Aristotle and Vico is for imagination to set forth notions of human prospects and human limitations whose ultimate meanings must be found out in the activities of the makers of the accounts. In such a manner, human beings make their nature.

For Vico, rational metaphysics enables us to find universals that are not accessible to poetry; in other words, philosophy enables us to extend our treatment of particulars in ways that poetry is incapable of doing. At the same time, he tells us that the sublime poet has a wisdom that is inaccessible to rational metaphysics. What Vico helps us overcome is what he calls "the conceit of scholars," "who will have it that what they know is as old as the world."[38] Persistence of this conceit leads one to treat the past as though the ancients had the same sort of wisdom as we possess; it comes from an ignorance of the poetic wisdom, or from an unwillingness to consider the ancient wisdom on its own terms. To understand that poetic wisdom is different from philosophic wisdom is not only to be humble before the unfulfilled prospects of the latter, but it is also to celebrate the meanings of poetic wisdom and to seek, through those meanings, added prospects for rational metaphysics. Following Vico, we may understand that we sometimes sense more than we know or can know. Indeed, what is captured in the attempt to know something through philosophic wisdom necessarily must change the experience as sensed; in striving to know, something of that which is sensed must be sacrificed. In knowing, an experience of a different sort comes to be known. We have pointed to the way in which Plato's philosopher, striving for virtue-in-itself, had to settle for the best conduct of which he was capable; and to Aristotle's poliscrafts-man, striving for happiness, yet mindful of the necessity of bettering the quality of his conduct instead of seeking an end beyond conduct. And what we found to be most enduring is their patience in the face of the unfinished character of human affairs, their willingness to take into account the precarious and the changing conditions which get in the way of knowing virtue-in-itself, or of achieving happiness. It is the integrity of their activity that is determined amidst the limitations of the human condition, not the particular outcome of that activity, which holds our attention. To Plato's and Aristotle's accounts of conduct Vico adds the insight that, in moving from poetic to rational metaphysics, we have made certain of our limitations even as we were striving to overcome them.

Vulgar poets with vivid sensations and strong imaginations create a world out of themselves while philosophers try to recreate the world that is there. Each world is a different one, but the difference does not lie solely in the *sense* of the one and the *intellect* of the other. Each in its own way shows something of the limitations of human conduct even as human conduct is being shaped by both sense and intellect making their ways with us. Vico likens the creations of vulgar poets to those of children:

> Children excel in imitation; we observe that they generally amuse themselves by imitating whatever they are able to apprehend. This axiom shows that the world in its infancy was composed of poetic nations, for poetry is nothing but

imitation. This axiom will explain the fact that all the arts of the necessary, the useful, the convenient, and even in large part those of human pleasure, were invented in the poetic centuries before the philosophers came; for the arts are but imitations of nature, and in a certain way 'real' poems (made not of words but of things). Men at first feel without perceiving, then they perceive with a troubled and agitated spirit, finally they reflect with a clear mind. This axiom is the principle of poetic sentences, which are formed by feelings of passion and emotion, whereas philosophic sentences are formed by reflection and reasoning. The more the latter rise toward universals, the closer they approach the truth; the more the former descend to particulars, the more certain they become.[39]

While we grow away from the ability to make vulgar poetry and toward the ability to do rational metaphysics, we are growing away from a way of being which we cannot fully regain. Yet it is in our nature to do so, and there is a certain gain in this development, to be determined by that which rational metaphysics brings into existence. In the same growing there is a loss, for whatever vulgar poetry brings into existence can no longer be made by rational metaphysics apart from the doing and making of human beings. We have created our poetry, our institutions, and our philosophy, even when we have not understood what we were doing. As we become capable of understanding what we have done by our philosophic wisdom, we are still making ourselves. Thus Vico's insight that human beings are capable of understanding the world of civil society because men made it makes us aware of our own limitations. One limitation is shown by our philosophic wisdom, for the poetic powers involved in making are largely lost as we find that we have gained the power to understand what has been made. Following this suggestion, Vico's work shows us the frustrations of living in a world which, when understood, is known to be the poetic, yet intelligible, creation that it is. The world that comes to be known is created by the understanding; and that world comes into being through sense and imagination working their way toward intelligence.

Vico writes about the sense in which human beings tried to employ their intelligence, but realized ends different from those which they had sought, in this way:

[In making the world of nations] men mean to gratify their bestial lust and abandon their offspring, and they inaugurate the chastity of marriage from which the families arise. The fathers mean to exercise without restraint their paternal power over their clients, and they subject them to the civil powers from which the cities arise. The reigning orders of nobles mean to abuse their lordly freedom over the plebians, and they are obliged to submit to the laws which establish popular liberty. The free peoples mean to shake off the yoke of their laws, and they become subject to monarchs. The monarchs mean to strengthen their own positions by debasing their subjects with all the vices of dissoluteness, and they dispose them to endure slavery at the hands of stronger nations. The nations mean to dissolve themselves, and their remnants flee for safety to the wilderness, whence, like the phoenix, they arise again. That which did all this was mind, for men did it with intelligence; it was not fate, for they did it by choice; not chance, for the results of their always so acting are perpetually the same.[40]

In such ways human beings have used their intelligence, but have not known fully what they did or made; using their intelligence has resulted in consequences different from those which they had sought and yearned for. Human beings have chosen and have received what they did not choose. What they have made is not what they have tried to make. What they have imagined is not the way things are, but imagining has had its part in the world that has been made. They have not been in control of their destinies even though in making themselves and their institutions, they have tried to do so by using their senses and their intellects.

Vico argues that human beings have made the world which they try to sense, remember, and understand; yet in their sensing, remembering, and understanding they are making something else of that world. This means that they are making themselves not exactly as their hearts and minds desire. Vico argues that human beings have indeed used their intelligence; yet in doing so they have not known fully what they thought they knew; unintended consequences resulted from their actions. What human beings have imagined is not exactly what things are; at the same time, those imaginings made a difference in the world that was created. Human beings have not been able to control their destinies, even while what they did contributed to what human beings have become. Thus our imaginings and our reasonings limit us, even as they create us; to admit that we are limited, yet unable to cease imagining and reasoning is to strive for further limiting and further creating. What this means is that we have no aims that are not our own; at the same time there is no assurance that we shall realize these aims. If Vico is correct, we have no firm ground for optimism about the prospects of the human condition. At the same time, we cannot escape the necessity of trying to use rational metaphysics to gain our heart's desire, to make of ourselves what we will.

Chapter 9

ROUSSEAU: HUMAN NATURE AND THE NECESSITY IN THINGS

The sense in which Jean-Jacques Rousseau's theory of education may be taken to be a theory of conduct is less apparent in his work than it is in writers such as Aristotle, Locke, and Vico. His theory of conduct is found in the context of discussions of human beings in their original nature and in their social, moral, and rational development. To illustrate the ideas of conduct in Rousseau's considerations of the relationship between human nature and human development, we take two hypothetical works, the *Discourse on the Origin and Foundation of Inequality of Mankind*[1] and *Emile*[2]. We call them hypothetical works because in the *Discourse*, Rousseau claims that he is "laying aside facts"[3] and writing a "hypothetical history of governments."[4] *Emile* is a fictional account of child-rearing, and the character Emile in the account is a hypothetical person. In the preface Rousseau suggests that what he has written is "less an educational treatise than a visionary's dreams about education."[5] This is not to say, of course, that facts are not taken into account by Rousseau; it is to say, instead, that in his use of literature, philosophy, science and other writings, Rousseau did not attempt to use facts for the purpose of writing a scientific treatise.

Rousseau was sensitive to the ancients' fascination with nature and with their efforts to develop arts which modified original human nature. He put this sentence from Aristotle's *Politics* on the title page of his

Discourse: "We should consider what is natural not in things which are depraved but in those which are rightly ordered according to nature." Rousseau responded to Aristotle's principle by trying to conceive of men as they were before they became depraved, as if men once lived in ways that were "rightly ordered according to nature." In the preface of his *Discourse*, Rousseau gives us a sense of what he means by the natural condition of the human soul in a striking figure, and points to the difficulty that arises out of the efforts to know men as nature formed them.

> How is it possible to know the source of the inequality among men, without knowing men themselves? And how shall man be able to see himself, such as nature formed him, in spite of all the alterations which a long succession of years and events must have produced in his original constitution, and how shall he be able to distinguish what is of his own essence, from what the circumstances he has been in and the progress he has made have added to, or changed in, his primitive condition? The human soul, like the statue of Glaucus which time, the sea and storms had so much disfigured that it resembled a wild beast more than a god, the human soul, I say, altered in society by the perpetual succession of a thousand causes, by the acquisition of numberless discoveries and errors, by the changes that have happened in the constitution of the body, by the perpetual jarring of the passions, has in a manner so changed in appearance as to be scarcely distinguishable; and by now we perceive in it, instead of a being always acting from certain and invariable principles, instead of that heavenly and majestic simplicity which its author had impressed upon it, nothing but the shocking contrast of passion that thinks it reasons, and an understanding grown delirious. But what is still more cruel, as every advance made by the human species serves only to remove it still further from its primitive condition, the more we accumulate new knowledge, the more we deprive ourselves of the means of acquiring the most important of all; and it is, in a manner, by the mere dint of studying man that we have lost the power of knowing him.[6]

The difficulty in philosophers' efforts to understand the nature of original men is that their efforts get in the way of their understanding. He goes on to say that he wants to lay aside all scientific treatises on the nature of man, which "teach us merely to consider men such as they have made themselves."[7] He distinguishes "natural men" (such as nature formed them) from "social men" (such as they have made themselves). Rousseau wants to understand what men were like in earlier stages of their existence in order to gain insight into their nature as they made themselves, and argues that the later, "social" condition of men is less natural then that of men as nature formed them.

Rousseau conceives of two kinds of inequality among men:

One which I call natural, or physical inequality, because it is established by nature, and consists in the difference of age, health, bodily strength, and the qualities of the mind, or of the soul; the other which may be termed moral, or political inequality, because it depends on a kind of convention, and is established, or at least authorized by the common consent of mankind.[8]

Does Rousseau mean to say that the two kinds of inequality (the one, "natural"; the other, "moral" or "political") are to be taken merely as *different* ways of being? Put differently, are natural conditions such that moral conditions necessarily stand in their way? There is a sense in which Rousseau sometimes writes as if "the natural" and "the moral" do oppose one another; or, as if the method by which one strives to understand the natural must somehow put aside the moral. It is as if natural man is amoral; and once moral considerations arise, men lose their true nature. Yet, Rousseau does not settle for the idea of calling natural men amoral, and social men moral. In the *Discourse*, he finds that men were involved in determining certain ways of being natural in the midst of the conditions which they were using to make themselves moral, social, and political. Or, more exactly, Rousseau writes about a natural condition prior to moral, social, and political considerations; as the story unfolds, Rousseau finds certain moral conditions that are "more nearly natural" than others. As an example, there is the kind of society which Rousseau thought was "the best for man" in the hypothetical history that is set forth in the *Discourse*. Man in his most primitive condition did not live under the social conditions which were best for the species. Rather, the best social conditions were found later in a less primitive society in which "a sense of morality began to insinuate itself into human actions . . . [and] that goodness of heart suitable to the pure state of nature by no means was suitable for the new society. . . ."[9] Rousseau says this, of the society which he imagined to have been "the best for men":

Thus, though men had become less patient, and natural compassion had already suffered some alteration, this period of the development of the human faculties, holding a just mean between the indolence of the primitive state and the petulant activity of egoism, must have been the happiest and most durable epoch. The more we reflect on this state, the more convinced we shall be, that it was the least subject of any to revolutions, the best for man, and that nothing could have drawn him out of it but some fatal accident, which, for the common good, should never have happened. The example of savages, most of whom have been found in this condition, seems to confirm that mankind was formed ever to remain in it, that this condition is the real youth of the world, and that all ulterior improvements have been so many steps, in appearance towards the perfection of individuals, but in fact towards the decrepitness of the species.[10]

While Rousseau insists that men lived in a "pure state of nature" prior to other kinds of societies, he also insists that the pure state, the most primitive one, was not "the best for men." Thus we are compelled by the story to hold that men have made different natures of themselves as their moral, social, and political conditions have changed. In taking action, they have in a sense made those conditions even while the conditions were making them. In Rousseau's eyes, "nature" in Aristotle's *Politics* takes on different natures. We now understand a sense in which things which are "rightly ordered according to nature" are to be sought amongst the new natures which men make of themselves. Man, in learning how to live in different social contexts, has literally made different natures; what he is cannot be torn away from his social context without doing violence to his nature. If, in modern times, we are living in a social context that is characterized by a "passion that thinks it reasons, and an understanding grown delirious," let us be mindful that this condition is now a part of our nature, a condition inextricably connected with our social being. Now it is in our nature to be this way, so that we can speak of a changed social nature.

In the following passage, Rousseau appears to be writing about two senses of nature:

> [In going from the state of nature to the social state] he will perceive that, the mankind of one age not being the mankind of another ... he will find himself in a condition to understand how the soul and the passions of men by insensible alterations *change as it were their very nature*; how it comes to pass, that in the long run our wants and our pleasures seek new objects; that, original man vanishing by degrees, society no longer offers to the sage anything but an assemblage of artificial men and factitious passions, which are the work of all these new relations, and have no foundation in nature.[11]

One sense of nature here is "original nature," that in which the nature of "artificial" men "has no foundation." Yet he does acknowledge that artificial men have a nature of their own. In holding that one condition, "the real youth of the world," was the best for men, he simply holds that human beings have taken on a social nature which they did not have in their original condition. To be more accurate, we must say that they have taken on several social natures, one of which was the best for them, but the ones taken on since the best one have made them more depraved. In any case, whether we talk about "insensible alterations," "original man vanishing by degrees," or "some fatal accident" of human beings, the position taken by

Rousseau is clear: despite the fact that human activities of making and trying to understand what they have made get in the way of understanding what is "rightly ordered according to nature", human beings have "made themselves," at times for better and at other times for worse. The way we understand how they have made themselves and what they have made of themselves is to be determined by our hypothetical accounts of the activities. By their arts human beings have striven to do something with their original natures and with their acquired social natures. And by our conduct in interpreting the consequences of those activities in literature, philosophy, and customs, we try to understand what has been made and done.

On the surface Rousseau differs from Vico in that Rousseau denies that he is writing a scientific treatise ("let us begin ... by laying aside facts"[12]), while Vico attempts to construct a "new science" of the materials by which the original nature of human beings worked itself into a "civilized", rational nature. Yet, if we look beneath the surface, we can detect a sense in which Rousseau's original men possess something akin to Vico's poetic metaphysicians; and we can detect a sense in which Rousseau's social men possess something akin to Vico's rational metaphysicians. Yet there is a difference in their conceptions of these: Vico saw the development from poetic to rational, not as a change from "natural" to "depraved," but as a change from one way of being in the world to another. Each conducts itself in ways appropriate to its nature. Like Vico, Rousseau saw the change from original nature to social nature as a change that needed to be interpreted in terms of each nature. In addition, however, he saw the social natures that developed as taking on characteristics that finally were "less good," in a sense "less natural," than the original nature. Thus Rousseau shared something in common with Vico's idea that early human beings were essentially different in nature from later human beings. Rousseau put it this way: "We shall not be obliged to make man a philosopher before he is a man."[13] At the same time, there remains a sense in which Rousseau's distinction insists that a man in the original state is better than a philosopher. Vico's poetic metaphysician was different from, but not taken to be superior to or inferior to his rational metaphysician: as poet, the former excels; as philosopher, the latter excels. "The savage lives within himself," Rousseau writes, "whereas social man, constantly outside himself, knows only how to live in the opinion of others."[14] The consequence of this, for social man, is that he becomes so dependent on others for their judgment of him that "we have nothing but a deceitful and frivolous exterior, honor without virtue, reason without wisdom, and pleasure without happiness."[15] This is the consequence of human beings having been drawn too far out of the state that was best for them; this is the social behavior exemplified in what he earlier called "the decrepitness of the species."

In the preface to the *Discourse*, Rousseau had said that he was "considering what we should have become, had we been left to ourselves."[16] Thus he gives voice to a kind of longing to be let alone. Yet it is clear that social conditions arose that got in the way of what we should have become, and we made something else of ourselves, expressed as "the petulant activity of egoism." Decrepit social man, unlike the indolent primitives or those human beings who lived in the state of their youth that was best for them, has suffered from *perfectibility*, Rousseau writes. The capacity to make progress "produces his discoveries and mistakes, his virtues and his vices,"[17] so it is clear that we make ourselves along with it. Yet, "in the long run," Rousseau goes on, this capacity "renders him both his own and nature's tyrant."[18] What is against nature is against our own best nature, against "what we should have become."

Rousseau's aim, in *Emile*, is to pursue a hypothetical course of education with a hypothetical child. In finding continuity with the hypothetical history of the *Discourse*, we may think of Rousseau striving to create conditions in which something of Emile's original nature is transformed into the kind of social, moral, and rational man who is not "nature's tyrant". Another way of putting it is to say that Rousseau's conception of the human beings who lived in the state that was "best for man" in the *Discourse* provides a useful clue to what Emile should become.

In *Emile*, the contrast between "the original state of man" and "the spirit of society" continues to be made. Emile's tutor creates a little society especially for Emile, in order to protect him from the larger society which would teach him only to live according to the opinion of others. In referring to the ends of education that are available to Emile's tutor, Rousseau puts the contrast betwen nature and society in this way:

> Forced to combat nature or the social institutions, one must choose between making a man or a citizen, for one cannot make both at the same time. . . . Good social conditions are those that best know how to denature man, to take his absolute existence from him in order to give him a relative one and transport the *I* into a common unity, with the result that each individual believes himself no longer one but a part of the unity and no longer feels except within the whole.[19]

In what sense is Rousseau "forced to *combat* nature or the social institutions"? Rousseau writes, "On leaving my hands, he will, I admit, be neither magistrate nor soldier nor priest. He will, in the first place, be a man. All that a man should be, he will in case of need know how to be as well as anyone; and fortune may try as it may to make him change place, he will always be in his own place."[20] In saying this he plainly intends to combat those elements of society which would train Emile for a particular calling. Yet it is Rousseau's aim, in educating Emile to be a man, to make him a social being as well. Indeed, after one is transformed from "original man" to "social man," one *must* be a social being. And if one is a man and a social being, he will also be a citizen. We shall see later that Rousseau's idea is to make Emile a citizen also; it is important to recognize that his manhood comes first in such a way that all else follows. This is the principle of development which Rousseau follows.

We have already suggested that the course of education set forth in *Emile* brings to mind the course of human history earlier set forth in the *Discourse on Inequality*. Emile begins "as nature made him"; in some sense, he is natural; through his education, he must become a man, moral, rational, and social. Again we find Rousseau writing of what is natural, and again we find him transforming the natural into the social, the moral, and the rational. Emile's nature, as was human nature in the *Discourse*, is transformed.

Yet it is not in opposition to the social, moral, and rational conditions of man that Rousseau brings up Emile. Instead, these conditions are part of the necessity of things. The question is not whether Emile shall remain "natural", as if there were only one possible nature for human beings. It is, what kind of moral, social, and rational man shall he become, what sort of nature shall he eventually take on. Again, as in the *Discourse*, Rousseau finds that "what is best for (this particular) man" is a condition which embodies certain moral, social, and rational qualities. Natural Emile must face the necessity of things and grow out of his original nature into a different one. Essentially, then, Rousseau shows us two senses of nature in Emile: one, "such as nature formed him," and another, such as he is formed through education, "such as he made himself." In the following lines, Rousseau brings together these two senses of nature:

> Nature wants children to be children before being men. If we want to pervert this order we shall produce precocious fruits which will be immature and insipid and will not be long in rotting. We shall have young doctors and old children. Childhood has its ways of seeing, thinking, and feeling which are proper to it. Nothing is less sensible than to want to substitute ours for theirs.[21]

Rousseau's care in distinguishing "the ways of childhood" from "the ways of men" shows us that he wanted to honor the ways of childhood, not only for their own sake, but for the sake of the ways of men as well.

"Childhood is reason's sleep,"[22] Rousseau tells us. He shows us that childhood is also the sleep of memory, and of moral and social being. After taking care to argue that, before the "age of reason," children are not capable of judgment and have no true memory, Rousseau makes a fundamental qualification:

> I am, however, very far from thinking that children have no kind of reasoning. On the contrary, I see that they reason very well in everything they know that relates to their immediate and palpable interest. But one is mistaken about this knowledge, ascribing to them knowledge they do not have and making them reason about what they could not understand.[23]

In one sense, then, children are unable to reason as adults do who have reached the "age of reason"; but in another sense, the sense in which the child has its own ways of seeing, thinking, and feeling, children are indeed able to reason. There is a reason of childhood and a reason of adulthood; or, better put, we learn to make our nature as we conduct ourselves in certain ways of seeing, thinking, and feeling, and we thereby grow toward other ways of seeing, thinking, and feeling. Rousseau, in discussing one age of development, writes of moral ideas:

> See how we gradually approach moral notions which distinguish good and bad! Up to now we have known no law other than that of necessity. Now we are dealing with what is useful. We shall soon get to what is suitable and good.[24]

And on intelligence and the moral order in the same age:

> When they foresee their needs before feeling them, their intelligence is already quite advanced, and they begin to know the value of time. It is then important to accustom them to direct its employment to useful objects—but objects whose utility they can sense at their age and is within the reach of their understanding. All that depends on the moral order and on the practice of society ought not to be presented to them yet, because they are not in a condition to understand it. It is inept to demand that they apply themselves to things one tells them vaguely are for their own good (without their knowing what that good is) and to things they are assured they will profit from when they are grown up (without their taking any interest now in that alleged profit, which they would not be able to understand).[25]

To summarize: Rousseau sometimes writes as if children are arational, asocial, amoral. Yet his qualifications show that he means that they only lack *a particular kind* of reason, social sense, and moral concern, namely, that which they are capable of possessing when, at the "age of reason," they become adults. What they do have is a different kind of reason, social sense, and moral concern; lacking one kind, they possess another. It is this changing nature that we must recognize and try to understand.

Rousseau writes of Emile's social needs as he reaches the "age of reason":

> It (nature) chooses its instruments and regulates them according to need, not to opinion. Now, needs change according to the situation of men. There is a great difference between the natural man living in the state of nature and the natural man living in the state of society. Emile is not a savage to be relegated to the desert. He is a savage made to inhabit cities. He has to know how to find his necessities in them, to take advantage of their inhabitants, and to live, if not like them, at least with them.[26]

Emile's social needs, his moral needs, and his need for rationality are joined in a particular way as he reaches the "age of reason," even as his social, moral, and rational needs had sought fulfillment in different ways in the earlier ages of his development. As has been the case all along, Emile's nature is not opposed to reason, to morality, and to social being *per se*; his nature is only opposed to *certain ways* of being rational, moral, and social. All along, the aim has been to find a way of educating Emile, of making his nature such that these ways of being were integrated so as to form a human being of a particular kind.

It is important to understand that Rousseau's emphasis on a "reason of childhood" is fundamental to his conception of human nature and development. Yet it is equally important to understand that Rousseau believes that there is a "reason of adulthood" that is no less fundamental. In one sense, the child Emile is an incomplete person; in possessing "child reason" he lacks "adult reason"; we must recognize this if we are to understand Emile's developing nature. Rousseau does not wait until Emile is an adult to cultivate his reason; he cultivates it all along, even though education, in the early years, "consists not at all in teaching virtue or truth but in securing the heart from vice and the mind from error."[27] He is cultivating him as a child differently from the way he will cultivate him later on. In a sense, then, Emile is to be first a *full child* with his own capacities and limitations; he will not be a *full human being* until he has learned to follow nature's lead and become an adult with different capacities and limitations. Rousseau insists that we have different limitations and capacities as our nature develops; or, to put it another way, the limitations and capacities that we possess differently simply *are* our natures.

Later, when Emile is nearing adulthood, Rousseau writes, "I have made him feel that all the ideas which are salutary and truly useful to men were the first to be known."[28] Emile is capable of being convinced of this, according to the canons of adult reason, only when he has become an adult. Yet, in another and equally fundamental sense, the tutor has been convincing Emile of this throughout the course of his development. By learning how to gain an integrity that was appropriate to his developing nature all along the way, Emile enjoyed his earliest nature as "salutary" and "truly useful": it was good in itself, and proved its potentiality for further good by growing into a different nature which was good in itself. Thus, without knowing what he was doing, Emile learned to know by engaging in activities which were both good in themselves and good for learning to know. "By nature," Rousseau writes, "man hardly thinks. To think is an art he learns like all the others and with even more difficulty."[29] Emile is to be put "in the condition always to be master of himself and in all things to do his will, as soon as he has one."[30] Until he becomes an adult, Emile is an incomplete human being, a human being having different kinds of integrity in each age, each having its own nature. In a sense, he becomes several human beings, each *complete in itself*, but not complete in an ultimate sense. Emile has several *ages*.

Rousseau puts it in this way: "Each age, each condition of life, has its suitable perfection, a sort of maturity proper to it. We have often heard of a mature man, but let us consider a mature child."[31] Emile, who has "lived a child's life," has reached "the maturity of childhood" and has acquired "all the reason belonging to his age."[32] Yet it is clear that a mature child is not a mature adult; we are to consider him in both ways: as a mature child with the reason of his age, and as a mature adult with the reason of his age. In arguing that we have largely ignored the former, Rousseau asks us to keep the latter in mind as well. We are to expect some things of children *as* children, not for the sake of childhood only, but for the sake of the grownups whom children are capable of becoming. We may return to Rousseau's assertion that "childhood is reason's sleep." It is both a sleep in which the child's potential powers are resting and a sleep in which the child's actual powers are living a life of their own. Again, the actual powers have both a maturity of their own and a potentiality for the maturity of adulthood.

Yet we must not lose sight of the place of Rousseau's respect for childhood in his overall conception of development and its aims. It should be emphasized that Rousseau was not advocating that children be *let alone* in their development; in his mind, the ultimate end of development is always kept in mind while each proximate kind of nature is respected. And near the end of the book, when the grown-up Emile says to his tutor, "It is you, my master, who have made me free in teaching me to yield to necessity. Let it come when it pleases, I let myself be carried along without constraint,"[33] we understand that there is a necessity in things which has made captive Emile's will; at the same time, he has reached the "age of reason." What Emile wants to do is that which his reason shows him is what he must do. The "mature child" has become a "mature adult."

Hence Rousseau's political-moral truism that "society must be studied by means of men, and men by means of society"[34] expresses itself in a particularly striking way when Emile becomes a grown man. Rousseau held that in the best society the sovereign acts through its particular will, which also wants what its reason shows is good for it. This works if the sovereign truly expresses the general will and if individuals know what the general will wants and have learned to live according to its terms. Thus:

> Inasmuch as the individuals have subjected themselves only to the sovereign, and the sovereign authority is nothing other than the general will, we shall see how each man who obeys the sovereign obeys only himself, and how one is more free under the social pact than in the state of nature.[35]

Further, Rousseau writes that the laws give Emile the courage to be just and have taught him to rule himself. Rousseau's education according to nature has turned out to be a social education. It is in our nature to become social just as it is in our nature to become moral and rational. As our discussion of Emile's reason of childhood has shown that the child has rational powers, we may now say that Emile was learning to be social throughout his development at the same time. He was social in different ways at different ages in his development, and each of these ways is to be respected in itself and for the kind of social being Emile can become when he will learn how to rule himself.[36] It may be said truly that childhood is the "sleep of social existence" and the "sleep of morality" as well as "reason's sleep."

Near the end of the book, Emile says that he has decided to remain what his tutor made him.[37] In this there is a certain truism and a certain irony. If the development has taken place naturally Emile cannot be other than what his tutor made him. Emile has been learning all along to want what his tutor wants for him; his tutor has led him to believe that no other decision is possible. As Emile was both "reasoning" and "learning to be rational" throughout his development he must tell us at the end that he has decided to be what he was deciding all along: this is what it means to "yield to necessity." At the end he simply knows in one way what he was knowing in different ways all along.

Although we cannot rid ourselves of the necessity in things, we can be "made free" by learning to yield to it. In retrospect, Emile can know that he had learned to yield to necessity; but in prospect, he can only *be* what he is capable of becoming, which includes an inability to *know* what he can become. If we now consider Rousseau's admonition to "attach your heart only to imperishable beauty" [38] and his assertion, "the eternal laws of nature and order do exist,"[39] in the context of his conception of development, we find in him a kinship with Plato's philosopher striving for virtue-in-itself.

Knowing "imperishable beauty" and the "eternal laws of nature and order" is Rousseau's aim, but as in the sea-god Glaucus, what is eternal is obscured by its actual conditions. Yet we are compelled to believe in the existence of a true nature, Rousseau believes, which is revealed to human beings in their development. This development is understood through the way in which human beings come to know their nature; what is more, what it means to know our nature truly is to live in a certain way. For Rousseau, as for Plato's philosopher and for Aristotle's poliscraftsman, knowing is a sort of virtue: we know truly and live in goodness only when we know what is good for us and when we live according to that knowledge.

The question naturally arises: What claims does Rousseau make to knowing imperishable beauty and the eternal laws of nature and order? Let us recall that Rousseau's *Emile* is a hypothetical work, in which Emile's tutor acts as if he knows what is good for Emile. In a note which reveals much about the sort of work he considers *Emile* to be, Rousseau writes:

> One no longer studies, one no longer observes, one dreams; and we are gravely presented with the dreams of some bad nights as philosophy. I will be told that I, too, dream. I agree; but I give my dreams as dreams, which others are not careful to do, leaving it to the reader to find out whether they contain something useful for people who are awake.[40]

Thus Rousseau warns us that the account of Emile's development is the author's dream. Our understanding of the world we live in falls short of providing an exact knowledge of Emile's nature. Instead, we live in a world in which philosophers' dreams set forth accounts of things which fall short of true knowledge. As in Plato's accounts of philosophers striving for virtue-in-itself but not finding it, so in Rousseau's account in *Emile*: we are forced by the necessity of things to acknowledge our limitations and the difficulties they make for a savage who would live in a city, forced to be among others, but unlike them. Throughout Emile's education, Rousseau has tried to make him aware that his own nature is limited by the nature of the things that make up the "spirit of society"; that there are natural limits beyond which one cannot go, if one wants to remain true to his own nature. One understands and becomes what he is capable of becoming by learning not to overstep the bounds that are set by the relations established between himself and other things, between himself and other persons. Thus the power of reason develops by finding what is possible; the sense of morality works itself out by determining what one ought to do, consistent with what one sees, feels and thinks; and, finally, the rational, working hand in hand with the moral, determines the limits through which one becomes social. What it means to be rational, moral, and social may be considered as distinctions in thought; but they are necessarily related in the activities of living. The rational is not merely intellectual, but an activity of social and moral life, a way of conduct, and the nature of morality is found out in just the sort of rational and social activity that is worked out.

At the close of *Emile*, Rousseau has Emile face the reality that certain possibilities imagined for a genuine life of a savage living in a city are not open to him. Emile must live in a different social situation from the one that the eternal laws of nature and order declare are best for him. Emile is unable to create the kind of social context that would be the best one for a free human being. No state exists for Emile such as the hypothetical one Rousseau depicts in the *Discourse*, the one that was "best for man." *This* is the necessity in things to which Emile must yield.

With the passion of a young man in love, who believes very much in himself, in what he has become, Emile declares that he must live under the bonds of necessity:

> Rich or poor, I shall be free. I shall not be free in this or that land, in this or that region; I shall be free everywhere on earth. All the chains of opinion are broken for me; I know only those of necessity. I learned to bear these chains from my birth, and I shall bear them until my death, for I am a man.[41]

Rousseau responds by saying to Emile:

> I knew that when you looked at our institutions from close up, you would hardly gain a confidence in them which they do not merit. One aspires in vain to liberty under the safeguard of the laws. Laws! Where are there laws, and where are they respected? Everywhere you have only seen men's passions reigning under this name. But the eternal laws of nature and order do exist. For the wise man, they take the place of positive law. They are written in the depth of his heart by conscience and reason. It is to these that he ought to enslave himself in order to be free. The only slave is the man who does evil, for he always does it in spite of himself. Freedom is found in no form of government; it is in the heart of the free man. He takes it with him everywhere.[42]

Finally, then, "the eternal laws of nature and order" stand as *possibilities* of reason and morality, and would show us the true limits of social life, if we but knew them and were capable of acting in accord with what we know. But we do not know what it means to live according to the necessity of eternal laws. Our fate is otherwise; the necessity under which we live is very much of the world in which we find ourselves, rather than in a social existence that is "best for men," like the one in the *Discourse*. Rousseau recognized the necessity of the world in which Emile had to live, whatever the eternal laws of nature and of order say to him. Emile becomes a sort of tragic figure, who tried to respect the best that he had made of himself in learning to live with integrity in the world of necessity. Emile knew that he had to go on, seeking that which is "written in the depth of his heart by conscience and reason," holding forth the possibility that in the seeking, he would gain a kind of integrity.

Rousseau knows full well the limitations of existing social life, in which human beings are tempted away from the better possibilities of their nature. Even so, he has a keen feeling of the sense of needing to belong to the social system in which one lives. "Whatever country it is," he cries out to Emile, "he owes it what is most precious to man—the morality of his actions and the love of virtue."[43] One's society is one of the conditions that must be met in our search for morality and virtue. Emile cannot escape living in a society of some sort, even though his nature is not like that of others. We must live some place, if we are to be human. To those who say that we cannot live with integrity unless there are profound social changes that create a society worthy of the better nature of human beings, Rousseau shows us that, in the meantime, we must live. And in living, we must try to determine, in our small ways, what a society would be like that puts us in mind of the eternal laws. Rousseau's belief that there is a natural order which perfectly blends the rational and the social should not confuse us as to the place and function of that order. This natural order exists in the hypothetical world of the dreamer. Such an order suggests prospects for our reason and the spirit of society that are not now realized among any existing societies. In the meantime, Emile must make do by living with human beings, although he is not like them.

Rousseau's Emile puts us in mind of Plato's philosopher seeking virtue-in-itself. Each author strives to know and to act according to eternal verities. Each shows us how human beings are caught up in the necessity of things, that pursuing virtue-in-itself in Plato, and educating Emile coming to the age of reason, are not the eternal verities. Rather, what one achieves in each activity is a quality of conduct, a certain integrity of life. In order to maintain the natural, human integrity that has been hard-won in Emile's education, the most that one can do is suggested by Rousseau in these lines:

> The public good, which serves others only as a pretext, is a real motive for him alone. He learns to struggle with himself, to conquer himself, to sacrifice his interest to the common interest. It is not true that he draws no profit from the laws. They give him the courage to be just even among wicked men. It is not true that they have not made him free. They have taught him to reign over himself.[44]

The story of Emile's education is a drama, portraying the life of reason actively pursuing the moral life in an inescapably social context. Emile in his maturity is a human being whose rational, moral and social prospects are restricted by conditions that have not yielded to the better prospects of what it would mean to be human. What Rousseau shows us, as the drama closes, is not the human being whom Emile "should have become," but rather one who declares that he must settle for working out his destiny in a context whose moral conflicts remain very much with him. We have seen that Rousseau's conception of development has its tragic elements. No human beings exist "such as nature made them"; they exist "such as they have made themselves." And there is a certain paradox in the necessity of things, by which we can understand what our nature is only by making the nature that we try to understand.

Chapter 10

CONDILLAC'S NATURAL LOGIC

Condillac's treatment of the relation between *nature* and *conduct* provides the context for discussing his conception of conduct. Even though the theme has not been emphasized in the literature on Condillac's philosophy, it was suggestive to educational thinkers of his own time and endured to assert itself in the writings of later educational theorists.

One part of the theme says that nature gives us lessons; the other part says that if we learn the lessons which nature gives, we can conduct ourselves according to our nature and the nature of that which is given. To learn the lessons of nature is to learn the true lessons of conduct. This theme haunted contemporaries of Condillac (such as Rousseau) as well as his later followers (like Joseph Neef). It continued into the nineteenth century and found a place in the writings of certain educational theorists who wanted conduct to be empirical and natural, and who found a conception of empiricism and of nature in Condillac-like ideas for providing a rational ground on which conduct could be based.[1]

The aim here is to discuss Condillac's conception of the relation between nature and conduct as an educational matter. This is to say not only that the conception of nature-and-conduct had meanings for education. It is to say something more: Condillac's conception *is* an educational matter. The essential point of departure will be Condillac's *Logic*. This little work, written near the end of Condillac's life as a textbook of elementary logic to be used in schools, and prepared in response to a request from the government of Poland, first appeared in 1780.[2] The idea that logic as a study of the nature of conduct is essentially an educational matter stands out plainly in the *Logic*. In addition, his better-known *Essay on the Origin of Human Knowledge,* published in 1746, will be consulted.

Early in the *Logic,* Condillac says, "We shall not . . . begin this logic by definitions, axioms, or principles; we shall begin by observing the lessons which nature gives us."[3] He goes on to say that the "method of analysis" was learned from nature and that the method will be used to explain the origin of ideas or of faculties of the mind.[4] To help his readers get some sense of what he means by analysis, Condillac compares the activity of learning to direct our senses well to what children do when they acquire knowledge without the help of adults. The very fact that children do come to know is taken by Condillac as proof that nature teaches those who can pay attention to what it says. Children are sometimes capable of knowing because they have not yet learned the sorts of habits which would mislead them.

> They have then an art by which they acquire knowledge. It is true, they follow its rules without knowing it, but they follow them. We must therefore only make them remark what they do sometimes, in order to teach them how to do so always; and it will be found that we shall only teach them what they know how to do.[5]

The logic which we may learn from nature is implicit in the art exemplified in the activities by which children come to know without knowing how they do so. If we understood how they come to know, then we would possess the logic of knowing. We might say that it is only by engaging in certain activities, by conducting ourselves in certain ways, that we most fully can possess the logic implicit in the conduct of nature. It is not enough (even if it were possible) to *know* the logic without the conduct through which the logic is made explicit. We must experience the conduct if we are to understand its logic. To conduct ourselves *artfully* is not to reason; but we shall not reason "according to nature" unless we first conduct ourselves artfully.

After we have learned the reasons for our conduct, we must keep in mind a shortcoming: restricting reasoning to the rules of reason. This is to say that artful conduct (which is in accord with its rules of reason), along with a knowledge of its rules (but without self-consciously applying them), constitutes the "logic of nature," exemplified naturally, artfully, and logically. As Condillac puts it:

It would not be sufficient to conceive this logic, if we do not accustom ourselves to use the method which it teaches, and if that habit is not such that we can reason well without wanting to think of the rules, we shall not have the practice of the art of reasoning, we shall only possess its theory.[6]

We are now prepared to understand the significance of the "method of analysis" which Condillac had said was learned from nature and which then could be used to explain the origin of our ideas or our mental faculties. The way in which we conduct ourselves according to nature shows us the logic of things. By conducting ourselves according to nature we experience the way things are, and we learn the reasons why they are that way. As limited creatures, however, we cannot see all things simultaneously; yet, after seeing them in their natural order we will know how they exist, taken altogether. As Condillac puts it: "To analyze is . . . nothing else but to observe in a successive order the qualities of an object, so as to give them in the mind the simultaneous order in which they exist. This is what nature causes all of us to do."[7]

In the *Essay*, Condillac expressed his belief in the possibility that knowing could proceed in such a way that each truth prepares us for the next in such a way that no deliberate demonstration of its truth would be needed:

> In the exposition, as well as the investigation of truth, we ought to begin with the easiest ideas, such as are immediately derived from the senses; and afterwards to rise by degrees to more simple or more complex notions. I really believe that if we rightly comprehend the progression of truths, we should have no need to look for arguments to demonstrate them, the bare proposing them being sufficient; for they would follow one another in such order, that whatever a subsequent truth added to that which preceded, would be too simple to have need of any demonstration.[8]

Here we are reminded of "nature telling us" in the *Logic*. We have but to listen, and we can hear, and what we hear will be heard truly. Continuing, Condillac writes that "it is requisite we take notice of the order in which [a truth] might have been *naturally found*,"[9] if we are to communicate it in the correct order. He goes on: "*Nature itself* points out the order we ought to follow in the communication of truth; for if all our ideas come from the senses, it is manifest that the perception of abstract notions must be prepared by sensible ideas."[10]

Enough has been said to show that the method of analysis is a *general* method in the sense that it is appropriate for determining and finding truths, whatever subject matter is under investigation, and "the order" is to be found in nature. Condillac's *Logic* argues that we learn certain ways of conduct from nature. These give us reasons for so conducting ourselves. This is the essential meaning of the method of analysis, which he sets forth in his *Essay:*

> Our first aim, which we ought never to lose sight of, is the study of the human understanding; not to discover its nature, but to know its operations; to observe with what art they are combined, and how we ought to conduct them, in order to acquire all the knowledge of which we are capable. We must ascend to the origin of our ideas, we must unfold their formation, and trace them to the limits which nature had prescribed, to the end that we may fix the extent and boundaries of our knowledge, and new model as it were the whole frame of the human understanding.[11]

Here we can see that the *Logic's* emphasis on conduct, along with the idea that operations of nature are combined artfully, is clearly present in the earlier *Essay.* The point made there was not to *know nature* but to observe the artfulness of its operations, and to conduct ourselves according to that art in gaining further knowledge. In his later *Logic,* the significance of artful reason as a kind of conduct stands out plainly.

To summarize what has been said so far: Whether Condillac begins with the aim of studying logic or with the aim of studying the origins of human knowledge, the essentials are the artfulness of nature and the necessity of understanding the artfulness as a kind of conduct. This is a way of saying that an understanding of human knowledge and logic is an educational matter.

The meaning of Condillac's method of analysis, or way of understanding the artfulness of nature as a kind of conduct, is summarized in the *Essay:*

> Principles are only particular inferences which may serve to point out the most remarkable places through which we have passed; and that like the clue of a labyrinth, they are of no use when we want to proceed forward, but only facilitate the means of returning the way we came. Though they may be proper for easing the memory, and shortening disputes, by concisely pointing out those truths which both sides are agreed on; yet they generally become so vague and indeterminate, that if they are not used with caution, they multiply disputes, which then degenerate into a mere caviling about words. Hence the only means of acquiring knowledge, is to ascend to the origin of our ideas, to trace their formation, and to compare them under all their possible relations, which is what I call *to analyze.*[12]

The method of analysis is a general method, grounded in the nature of things. It is an educational method in the sense that it is the way of self-learning as well as a way of instructing others. And not only is it a "logical method"; it is the "method of logic," by which we conduct ourselves and others.

Yet there is another sense in which the study of the meaning of conduct is considered by Condillac. This is found in the consideration of those sciences which were taken to deal explicitly with the subject matters bearing on conduct, e.g., morality and politics. These are the subject matters which John Locke had placed under the heading of sciences of action.[13] Early in his *Essay*, Condillac argues that morals is a study susceptible to being known as exactly as geometry:

> It seemed to me that we might reason in metaphysics and in morals with as great exactness as in geometry; that we might frame as accurate ideas as the geometricians; that we might determine, as well as they, the meaning of words in a precise and invariable manner; in short that we might prescribe, perhaps better than they have done, a plain and easy order for the attainment of demonstration.[14]

One might argue that it is one kind of activity to direct our senses to the things of nature which make up the natural sciences, and another kind of activity to direct our senses to human actions which make up the sciences of morality. Yet in the *Logic* Condillac insists that "the morality of actions" falls under the senses.[15] He goes on to say that this is so because the morality of actions consists in the conformity of our actions with the laws, and that both actions and laws are visible.[16] While granting that laws are conventions which men have made, and that some laws are arbitrary, he insists that those laws which determine whether our actions are good or bad are not arbitrary.

Again, Condillac returns to the idea that the lessons which nature gives us are the lessons which we can learn. And here, in the case of those laws which determine whether our actions are good or bad, though men did make them, men did not make them alone: "Nature made them with us."[17] Our faculties can search through the labyrinth of arbitrary laws to the nonarbitrary ones, much as a child can learn to let his faculties have their ways with things and thereby learn naturally. To learn the laws which determine whether our actions are good or bad is to *"follow* those laws which are conformable to our natures."[18] The example of children observing and analyzing is appropriate again for the present context:

> Children are determined by their wants to be observers and to analyze; their growing faculties supply them with the means to be the one and do the other; nay in some manner they are forced to be observers, and to analyze so long

as nature leads them alone. But as soon as we begin to lead them ourselves, we forbid them every observation and analysis. We suppose they do not reason, because we do not know how to reason with them; and by waiting for an era of reason, which began without us, and which we delay with might and main, we doom them to judge only by our opinions, our prejudices and errors.[19]

Condillac's repeated example of children learning to observe and to analyze gives us some sense of what it would be like to know the logic of nature, even though we do not yet possess it.

The insistence that nature makes laws with us, expressed in the *Logic,* may be taken as an indication that Condillac had found a way of reducing the difficulty expressed in his discussion of "archetypal ideas" in the *Essay.* There he had said that to determine archetypal ideas, "those relating to human actions, to moral philosophy, jurisprudence, and the liberal arts,"[20] we must conduct ourselves differently from the way we do in determining the "ideas of substances." By the latter, he meant the knowledge obtained by analysis of properties of objects existing outside of human minds; our ideas of them are "no more than copies of what we perceive without ourselves."[21] In short, the truths of ideas of substances are derived from our sensations of external objects. On the other hand, archetypal ideas appeared to Condillac to "exist nowhere but in the mind of the first inventors." He continues:

> Human actions are combinations incessantly varying, of which it frequently concerns us to have some idea, before we have any patterns of them. Were we to frame our ideas of them only as experience instructed us, it would be oftentimes too late. We are therefore under a necessity of behaving here in a different manner; we unite or separate some simple ideas according as our fancy directs; or we adopt the combinations already made by others.[22]

This is a way of saying that the subject matters relating to human action are such that it is difficult to get sensations of their essential patterns. Our ideas, formed in the context of varying human actions, tend to be far removed from their true origins; or, in the vocabulary of Condillac's *Logic,* it is difficult to learn what nature tells us about archetypal ideas. Thus we are forced to act in this way:

> For the truth of [ideas of archetypes], it is sufficient that externally the combinations of them may possibly be such as they are in our minds. The idea of justice would be true, even if there were no such thing as a just action, because the truth of it consists in a collection of ideas, which does not at all depend on external objects.[23]

The question, whether or not the idea of justice in our minds is the one nature tells us is true, does not appear to be answered with the same sort of assurance that we enjoy about the idea of a right-angled triangle. Thus, while we might "reason," using the idea of justice with as great exactness as in geometry, we would not have the same sort of assurance about the truth of the idea of justice as we have about a theorem in Euclid. Now the essential appeal of Condillac's *Logic*, in regard to this question, lies in its insistence that nature makes laws with us; and that, "the faculties and wants of man being given, the laws are given themselves."[24] What remains, the faculties and the laws being given, is learning how to take what is given. To know the laws that are given by nature (in the *Logic*), and to have true ideas of archetypes (in the *Essay*), appear to be different ways of stating Condillac's object of knowledge.

To summarize Condillac's understanding of the sciences of conduct: His aim, stated both in the *Essay* and the *Logic,* was to subject them to the method of analysis. In the *Essay*, he has admitted differences between these sciences and those of mathematics and nature, which make it difficult to determine those ideas that are based on sensations of the actual objects making up the sciences of conduct. Yet, in the *Logic*, the aid we get from nature in making the laws to which moral conduct conforms is joined to human faculties in such manner that we can see the true moral laws in the midst of the merely arbitrary ones. It is as if his insistence that understanding begins with sensations has taught him to insist, further, that the natural way of understanding requires human faculties that are no less natural than the objects of the understanding. When nature *tells* us something, it is these faculties that are *told*. Thus all sciences, including the sciences of conduct, are *natural* sciences. They have a nature which is susceptible to analysis by the natural constitutions of human beings.

In examining Condillac's discussion of sciences of conduct, we return to the essential ideas of his *Logic:* (1) the meaning of logic is understood when we make explicit the artfulness of nature; and (2) this understanding is a sort of conduct. In experiencing the artfulness of nature, we are enabled to know the sciences of conduct. At the same time, this knowing is the very conduct by which nature makes laws with us. Whether we take Condillac's general method of learning and instructing, or the method he advocates for the study of the subject matters of conduct, we find certain meanings held in common. First, human beings are capable of feeling and acting in accord with these methods. It is in our nature to act and feel in these ways. Second, this nature is first implicit or unstated by human beings while it is experienced by them; and then it is made explicit or known only when they learn to ask what they have been doing. Third, that which is made explicit, and thereby becomes known, may be understood according to a method which Condillac calls the analytical method. Fourth, the analytical method is an art, insofar as it is undertaken without consulting its rules. Fifth, it is a logic insofar as it constitutes a way of doing things that may serve as a source of rules whenever we are unable to proceed artfully, or when we want to explain the way of doing things. Sixth, the analytical method as art-and-logic is not just a way of knowing, as if knowing takes place apart from doing. It is a way of doing as well, a way of conducting ourselves so that the arts and sciences genuinely will become a part of our conduct and not stand apart from it.

In returning to a central theme of Condillac's *Logic,* we must say that human beings are capable of taking the lessons which nature gives. This is possible because human beings are a part of nature. To know the lessons which nature gives, we must conduct ourselves in ways that express the logic by which the lessons get to be known.

Aristotle had the idea that art and education aim to fill nature's deficiencies. John of Salisbury thought that we should not forsake the ways of nature, yet added that virtue may be victorious over nature. Rousseau, while taken with the idea of understanding our original nature, understood also that we have made our nature, whatever our beginnings. For him the nature that we would take on, if we were only able to bring it into existence, is a kind of imagined idea by which we understand our actual conduct. Condillac's *nature* becomes more than an imagined idea in Rousseau's sense. It appears to take on a reality of its own which only awaits our understanding when we but *follow* it or *take* it as it is. Even though he qualifies this position in a reference to the laws which guide conduct by saying that nature "made them with us," the sense of nature which dominates Condillac's writings is one that appears to transform an idea into a reality. At times he almost reifies nature, making it appear to be something akin to Plato's virtue-in-itself. And when this happens to the idea of nature, it loses its sense of standing as a part *of* human conduct, even though *taking* nature must be a kind of conduct.

important for a theory of conduct: conduct is inescapably a social phenomenon. In fact, this is a truism for Dewey, but it needs to be stated just because education is commonly treated as if mind consisted of *mental states* existing apart from an environment, or as if emotion consisted of *feelings* existing apart from the social environment in which they are generated and to which they are a response. In saying, "society not only continues to exist *by* transmission, *by* communication, but it may fairly be said to exist *in* transmission, *in* communication,"[3] Dewey puts us in mind of Aristotle, of Cicero, and of Vico, in the importance they attach to commonplaces, to the *topics* which human beings of shared experience hold in common. Thus the interest in the conduct by which human dispositions take shape is joined to the idea that such conduct simply exists in experiences of transmission and communication with others. The nature of our conduct, the very quality of our experience, is found out in the ways in which we learn to conduct ourselves in common with others. What Charles Frankel wrote of Dewey's social philosophy may be said also of the place of conduct in Dewey's work: "Perhaps because Dewey's social philosophy is everywhere in his works, it it not easy to find it in any particular place."[4]

As Dewey emphasizes the social character of conduct, so he makes explicit the idea that conduct is moral in nature. "Morals are as broad as acts which concern our relationships with others,"[5] he writes. In this he shares the ancient wisdom according to which the acquiring of virtues is a way of acting. If we come to possess the virtues it is as a consequence of and a part of the very activities by which we are trained and in whose midst we take thought. Plato's philosopher seeking virtue-in-itself and Aristotle's poliscraftsman, each in its own way, illustrate what Dewey had in mind when he wrote: "To possess virtue does not signify to have cultivated a few nameable and exclusive traits; it means to be fully and adequately what one is capable of becoming through association with others in all the offices of life."[6] Charles Frankel captures well the spirit of Dewey's philosophy when he wrote: "He saw it as a civic enterprise."[7] Not a "bag of virtues," but a whole character of a certain kind, one that is shaped in conduct, is what it means to possess virtue. Dewey's continuity with the essential meaning of conduct that we have been discussing, the idea that conduct is inescapably social and moral, is put neatly in this sentence: "The moral and social quality of conduct are, in the last analysis, identical with each other."[8]

Dewey shares Vico's sensitivity to the limited place taken by intelligence in determining rules and social conditions, holding that the place of intelligence is small in gaining the consequences we desire as compared to its large place in working out the means by which consequences are sought. At the same time he shares with Aristotle and with Locke the idea that the possibility exists that our intelligence may make a difference in things. "To take advantage of conditions after they have come into existence is one thing," Dewey writes; "to create them for the sake of an advantage to accrue is quite another thing,"[9] he goes on. Clearly the former has been and remains the prevailing kind of activity; yet in holding forth the prospect that the latter is a possibility, Dewey strives for intelligence to take a larger place in the nature of things. While, for the most part, "the history of mind ... registers ... what has happened after it has happened,"[10] Dewey argues that it is not necessary for the truth in such a claim to seal our fate. Rather, it is one condition to be met if we strive to reflect and to turn our reflections into action as we work against the soporific claims of the fatalists. "The poignancy of situations that evoke reflection lies in the fact that we really do not know the meaning of the tendencies that are pressing for action,"[11] he writes, as a way of arguing that the existence of our tendencies is one thing, their meaning another.

Our efforts to survive, to seek pleasure, to find meaning, and to be social, are facts of social existence. The ways we survive or fail to do so, the ways we find pleasure or fail to do so, the nature of the meanings we find, the quality of our social existence: these are what need to be found out, and the means by which we take action in finding them, together with the outcomes gained, constitute the very meanings that are brought into existence. "While the stuff of belief and proposition is not originated by us,"[12] but rather stands among the givens of Rousseau's "origins" and "acquired" nature, what we take and what we do with what is taken become part of whatever nature we acquire and constitute the means and eventually the meanings of our beliefs and propositions. All of this is a way of saying that reflection and deliberation, all the activities of intelligence, are a search for an outcome which cannot be known prior to the activities by which we strive to know. "Deliberation is a work of discovery,"[13] Dewey writes. Yet it is clear that it is not a discovery of something that existed prior to the seeking. Discoveries are experiments in doing in which the outcomes of the doing are something *done* and what is done remains as a later part of the activity, not something which exists apart from the activity.

Here Dewey's thinking is a continuation of the drama of Plato's philosophers, who sought virtue-in-itself which would be free from all activity, yet who had to settle for an activity whose nature would be the achieved end. Dewey's investigator, like Aristotle's poliscraftsman, has to recognize not only the necessity of doing in order to find out the meanings of "the stuff of belief and proposition"; at the same time, he has to understand that having an end for an activity is a "*means* in present action."[14] "Ends," he writes, "are in no sense ends *of* action. In being ends of *deliberation* they are redirecting pivots *in* action."[15] Here is a restatement of Aristotle's notion that our investigations begin with an idea of "that which is to be" and, in our strivings, we aim to alter the nature of what we are doing by following the lead of the idea. As in Aristotle's idea that we do not investigate the nature of virtue in order to know what it is, "but in order that we may become good,"[16] Dewey's characterization of ideas as "anticipations of some continuity of an activity and a consequence which has not yet shown itself,"[17] points to the possibility of determining some good which, like Aristotle's virtue, is a quality of life in conduct. And in saying that ideas are "tested by the operation of acting upon them,"[18] Dewey reiterates, in his own way, what Aristotle was seeking when he said that when we carry our inquiry (into the nature of virtue) into conduct, it is "to ask how we are to act rightly."[19] For Aristotle, "becoming good," "acting rightly"; for Dewey, finding a consequence "which has not yet shown itself," by testing our ideas; there is the sense that a quality of life different from that with which we began the inquiry may be brought into existence, may be actualized in conduct. Both begin with "what is known to us"; neither believes that "what is knowable in itself" is a possible outcome of deliberations in matters of conduct. Instead, the most we may gain is "better conduct," a quality of social existence which may stand as a "conducted practice" that is "better" as a consequence of deliberation.

Dewey's empiricism is true to Aristotle's idea that each of the virtues embodies a kind of experience that is its own. Each virtue stands different from the others, yet all are needed in striving for the highest good. Dewey's counterpart of Aristotle's plurality of virtues is put neatly in this sentence: "Immediate Empiricism postulates that things—anything, eveything, in the ordinary or nontechnical use of the term 'thing'—are what they are experienced as." [20] Dewey goes on to say, "if one wishes to describe anything truly, his task is to tell what it is experienced as being."[21] Now if we take "thing" here to refer to any kind of experience characterized by Aristotle as embodying one of the virtues, "prudence" is one kind of thing, "scientific knowledge" another kind. Dewey, following Aristotle, would argue that what prudence is experienced as is one thing; it is one of the kinds of things that "admits of variation," and has no end outside its own activity. What Aristotle calls scientific knowledge is another kind of thing, an experience of demonstrating a truth from other truths. In each virtue what things are experienced as is just what they are; by letting the subject matter of each have its way with us, we are led to have an experience of a certain kind. At the same time, it is we who are experiencing the things with which we strive to be prudent, and the things with which we strive to gain scientific knowledge. In each, we are a part of the action, not apart from the action. Thus the way things are experienced becomes the conduct for which each virtue takes its name.

In characterizing what human beings are capable of receiving in education, Dewey elaborates on the meaning of better conduct gained, both for the individual and for the social medium in which and through which education takes place. Dewey refers to the old saying that one must not only be good, but be "good for something." He goes on to put it this way: "The something for which a man must be good is the capacity to live as a social member so that what he gets from living with others balances with what he contributes."[22] Thus the experience with others is a giving and a taking which aims to alter the quality of the life that is mutually shared. "What he gets and gives as a human being . . . is not external possessions, but a widening and deepening of conscious life—a more intense, disciplined, and expanding realization of meanings."[23] Dewey's ideal here requires what was missing in the larger society in which the grown-up Emile realizes he had to live; living with others, Emile was so unlike them that he knew he would be estranged from them. The virtues possessed by Emile were his alone and, although he hungered to share them with others, it was his very possession of certain virtues which made him a stranger to others. It was the very quality of his existence which made him homeless, even while he realized that he had to live somewhere.

Like Rousseau, Dewey recognizes the difficulty in finding a home in which one can live with integrity; yet Dewey does not hold to Rousseau's near-fatalism. As we have seen in Rousseau's *Discourse*, it is as if the ways in which human beings have made themselves have brought them to a mode of social existence which is naturally destructive of the better nature which human beings once possessed in the age that was best for them. Because of the nature of this social existence, human beings are incapable of joining together in ways that provide the kind of "balance" Dewey has in mind. To put it in another way, for Rousseau, the uncertainties of social existence acknowledged by every one of our thinkers are so much a part of our nature that we cannot alter the conditions for the better, we cannot make them balance what we get with what we contribute in such a way that Emile can find a home. It is not merely the case that Emile will be estranged; what is more, he cannot grow in ways that will ameliorate the estrangement.

While Dewey admits the existence of conditions that tend to estrange us from one another and from the better prospects of our nature, he writes of the possibility of altering those conditions, of putting them to work to ameliorate the human condition towards gaining the balance he thinks is desirable. "*If* change is genuine, if accounts are still in process of making, and if objective uncertainty is the stimulus to reflection, then variation in action, novelty and experiment, have a true meaning."[24] In short, "objective uncertainty" is a fact of life; but a desire to deal with uncertainty is also a fact of life. The meaning of the facts is yet to be determined, and the meaning is found out through the means by which we strive to determine the desired balance. Dewey, stimulated by uncertainty, is Aristotle's poli-scraftsman wanting "to have desire count as a factor, a force."[25] Dewey sees the possibility of an Emile who works to make a place to live when he is unable to find one. Rather than an Emile who has been made free by yielding to necessity, Dewey's Emile would strive to take what is necessary and work to alter the character of his social context. He would realize that the most important necessity is that we must make our freedom, if we are to be free. "To foresee future objective alternatives and to be able by deliberation to choose one of them and thereby weight its chances in the struggle for future existence, measures our freedom,"[26] is the way Dewey puts it.

Dewey admits that we cannot know in advance the degree to which we may expect control over future experience, or the fate of our ideas when they are tested in action. Yet we do know that, unless we learn how to gain control in some measure, we will not alter the necessity of things. "Freedom is the 'truth of necessity,'" Dewey says, "only when we use one 'necessity' to alter another."[27] The necessity of living in some place is a fact of social existence; but the judgment of Emile that wherever he lives he can trust only the truth that is found in his heart rather than any social relations he may develop does not take seriously an idea like Dewey's that the meaning of necessity is determined by taking the necessity as a condition to be acted upon with the aim of altering the quality of experience. The necessity is to be taken as a *necessary condition* rather than one sufficient to determine the quality of experience. When Dewey writes, "Men have to *do* something to the things when they wish to find out something,"[28] he does not mean that the thing found out is already present. In conduct, the doing contributes to making what is found; it takes its place in bringing into existence a way of conduct which then exists as a fact of social existence. This is the essence of an empiricism which insists that things are what they are experienced as: if, in the doing, we bring into existence a new way of conduct, we have experienced what we made. We aim to experience a new way of conducting ourselves; to aim for it is to desire it. Whether it *will* be experienced is an empirical question, and cannot be answered except by striving to bring into existence the conduct that we desire.

Dewey's discussion of the way in which a social environment may be artificial, "but its action in response to ours is natural not artificial,"[29] in one sense makes explicit what is implicit in Rousseau's struggles to distinguish between "original men" who were natural, and "social men" who are artificial. Rousseau had realized that human beings, in degenerating from natural to artificial creatures, had been involved in making their nature; thus it is in action that our "nature" is to be found. In our social context, we cannot know anyone in an "original natural condition"; we can only know human beings as they have made themselves. Again, Rousseau takes this not to be merely a "fact of social existence," but a worsened human condition which has taken such hold of our destiny that Emile cannot find a place to live with a natural integrity that matches his own. Dewey, on the other hand, takes behavior in "artificial" social conditions to be "natural" in the sense that it is our social nature to respond to others even as they are responding to us. This is to say that certain activities of human beings just are "facts of social existence," rather than artificial conditions which, in the necessity of social conditions, prevent us from being "natural." Further, we may have a hand in determining the meaning of these facts. "In language and imagination," Dewey writes, "we rehearse the responses of others just as we dramatically enact other consequences. We foreknow how others will act, and the foreknowledge is the beginning of judgment passed on action."[30] In such manner is our conduct shaped, not merely by others' responses to our conduct, but by our anticipations of the ways in which others will respond and by our anticipations of the ways in which we will respond to them. So far Rousseau would agree. Yet in the actual ways in which we will conduct ourselves, and in the prospect that the conduct may make a difference in our fate, Dewey sees the prospect that our conduct may at least ameliorate the conditions that we make for ourselves.

For Emile no home available to him can be good for him. Where Dewey continues by saying, "We know *with* them (others); there is conscience,"[31] we see the prospect of a shared conduct by which the knowing with others will have altered the conduct for the better. This is a different prospect from that of Emile living with others but not like them, and incapable of sharing a conscience with them that stands for a "good" conduct for all concerned. To put it differently, while Rousseau would agree with Dewey that "the *meaning* of native activities is not native; it is acquired,"[32] he would disagree with Dewey's idea that when the acquired meanings go into action they may become instrumental in altering conduct for the better. And Rousseau probably would agree with Dewey "that our judgments are themselves facts which have consequences and that their value depends upon *their* consequences."[33] Yet Rousseau appears to emphasize only the *having* of consequences, as if consequences are and only can be *had*, while Dewey holds forth the prospect that our judgments may *make* certain consequences happen, and that it is imperative to strive for "expanding realizations of meaning," for the good of what is human in our nature. Such meanings can be brought into existence where social conditions not only are necessary, but are put to use to alter another necessity.

In Dewey's thought, we see something akin to Pindar's striving to gain the victor's prize, and similar to the tragic figures who learned that we shall not understand our limitations unless we strive to overcome them.

This appears in Dewey's idea that what we strive to overcome is the hold the social environment will have over us unless we take action to overcome certain of its features. Yet he does not strive against what is social *per se*; he works to put certain social elements in cooperation with others with the aim of ameliorating the necessity in things to which Emile yielded. At the same time it is clear that Dewey is far from being optimistic about the prospect of ameliorating the necessities in things. While he argues that it is no less natural to attempt to use intelligence in aiming to alter our conduct than it is to act as if the limits of our conduct are set by the very nature of things, he does not fail to recognize the place held by instinct and habit in determining our activities. He writes, "Man continues to live because he is a living creature not because reason convinces him of the certainty or probability of future satisfactions and achievements. He is instinct with activities that carry him on."[34]

It must not be forgotten that, by taking thought, one is a different kind of living creature from one who fails to take thought. By thinking, we are alive in a way that seeks different possibilities in things, even though we may be humbled when the possible fails to actualize. In referring to humility, Dewey says that "it is the sense of our slight inability even with our best intelligence and effort to command events; a sense of our dependence upon forces that go their way without our wish and plan."[35] This humility shares something with Plato's human soul in the *Phaedrus*, striving to see where the gods go, but again falling short of virtue-in-itself and having to settle for seeing "in part" and in part "seeing not." Dewey has a more modest aim than Plato's charioteer. Dewey aims merely for a kind of growth which might improve the quality of lives which human beings share in common, rather than seeking virtue-in-itself. Yet Dewey's humility shares with the striving of the charioteer the conviction that the actions taken *are* the meaning of the striving; in our humility we aim to go on, even though we have not gained all the meaning we sought. Again, in referring to humility, Dewey says: "Its purport is not to relax effort but to make us prize every opportunity of present growth."[36] Even in failing to gain the good that was sought, Dewey argues, the experience of failing may constitute a kind of growth, if it can be taken as an opportunity for seeking a different good. In any case, the judgment that we have failed is itself a fact of life whose consequences we may continue to determine in striving for a different good.

Chapter 12

MAKING OUR NATURE: A NECESSITY IN CONDUCT

Our writers on conduct hold one essential idea in common. It has its origins in Aristotle's predecessors, was stated in its classic form in Aristotle's writings on the poliscraft, and has been restated in various forms from Aristotle to Dewey. In Aristotle's clear distinction between scientific knowledge and prudence we find a classic statement of this idea. In scientific knowledge, we demonstrate, Aristotle thought. In prudence, we do things and our activities are just what we do; there is nothing apart from the doing to demonstrate. The distinction is overlooked when advocates of scientism attempt to submit subject matters which bear on prudence to the standards of scientific knowledge. The claim that one virtue is superior to the other virtues, or that the standards of one science may be applied to all the others, does not acknowledge the significance of Aristotle's plurality of virtues. His conception of prudence as the virtue which has no end outside the activity which constitutes virtuous action is the classic statement about conduct which educational theory cannot do without.

Aristotle's pluralism demands a careful empiricism: we begin our investigations by taking into account the nature of the matters to which we subject ourselves. At the same time, the integrity of our investigations in matters of conduct is determined by the ways in which we shape the nature of these matters. When opinions held with integrity are the best which subject matters of conduct are capable of yielding, then it is a presumption against the nature of the subject matter to expect scientific knowledge. Action through which we settle for opinions is not just "aimless activity"; rather it is an activity that strives for the highest conduct of which one is capable in the circumstances in which he finds himself. While such activity is not capable of yielding scientific knowledge, and thus differs from Plato's virtue-in-itself, it shares with Plato's aim the effort to bring the best into existence. In the midst of the subject matter of conduct, we strive to bring to pass the best that is in us. In conduct, we are not merely in the subject matter, but we are a part of the subject matter that we are trying to shape.

A strong functionalism is evident here. In *After Virtue*, Alasdair MacIntyre makes the point that in the Aristotelian tradition to call something good is to say that it has a specific purpose or function.[1] We have discussed this idea as found in Aristotle's *Nicomachean Ethics* where he says the goodness of one who has a function to perform is found in the function.[2] Clearly, Dewey's functionalism also is an expression of this idea: Dewey said that one must not only be good, but be good for something. Aristotle and Dewey insist that the quality of the good is determined in the experience of living as a social being.

Certain activities of human beings, Dewey says, are "facts of social existence"; to call certain activities good is to illustrate a sense in which Aristotle's "goods" have a specific function. It remains for the quality of the good to be worked out in experience. Aristotle shows us that the aim is to do well, to act so that we continue to do well. The aim is for our doings to grow into further doings whose quality is different from (and better than) the earlier doings. We have seen this idea expressed in Dewey's thinking; for him, "better doings" are signs of growth.

In addition to Aristotle and Dewey, we recall others for whom there was no end apart from conduct, who held that the ends of conduct were made in conduct itself. The ancient orators insisted on the strength of commonplaces and the necessity of finding their meanings by learning to conduct ourselves as did those from whose experience the commonplaces emerged. Vico argued on behalf of an education in the arts and topics of conduct, and came to believe that human beings have made themselves as social beings. This means that they understand themselves insofar as they construct something of the world which they have made through poetic and rational metaphysics. The difficulty in understanding ourselves is that we are making ourselves even as we are trying to understand what we have made; thus we are forced by the necessity in things to attempt to understand what we are making as well as what we have made. Rousseau agonized over a similar necessity, though couched in a different context.

Understanding our original nature is difficult because we have taken on a different nature which gets in the way of understanding what we were like in our origins. He shares with Vico a sense of the significance of trying to understand that which is in the process of taking shape even while we have some part in the shaping. Vico and Rousseau share with Aristotle and Dewey the idea that we are responsible for our conduct, and that only by the actions through which our conduct takes shape do we make the nature that we are trying to understand. Thus not only does our knowing come by doing, but the quality of what is done is more important than what we know. We may even say that what we do is what we know. To take this idea seriously is to hold that what is most important is the activity by which principles are taken into account, rather than the virtues, *as* principles of knowledge. Plato had Socrates say that the virtues are forms of knowledge, that the virtues are principles. Aristotle held, instead, that the virtues *cooperate* with principles. This essential insight into the possibility of working to improve conduct reappears in various forms in the work of our thinkers.

The work of some of our writers, while expressing keenly the sense that theory of education is a theory of conduct, has in it a certain ambiguity. In a large part, these writers hold the idea that understanding in general and thinking in particular are matters of action from which conduct comes, or which simply and necessarily *are* matters of conduct. Here is a sort of "empirical wisdom" which shows us that by studying what human beings actually do and by striving to improve our conduct on the basis of this wisdom, we have to work in the midst of what Locke called the "various and unknown humours, interests, and capacities of men." In doing this, we recognize that our common sense often is all-too-common. Yet only out of its context may we hope to determine a different sense, one that is less common and of greater value. As examples, Plato's philosopher is engaged in a joint investigation with others; Augustine portrays the way to Wisdom as a way of conduct; Clement believes that we must strive for innocence by trying to be like children; John of Salisbury learns the arts of conduct by engaging in humanistic studies in order to take on the conduct they stand for; for John Locke, learning certain habits of conduct takes priority over children's studies; and Condillac thinks that we must learn to act in accord with natural laws of conduct. Yet a certain ambiguity is found in their work. For all their sensitivity to the necessity of doing, each is tempted by the prospect of principles of conduct which would stand beyond particular acts of conduct, if only we knew them.

Plato's philosopher seeks virtue-in-itself. Augustine wants to find God by dying to the world of human conduct. Clement's childhood innocence is pure, so lacking in this-wordly modes of behavior that it appears to be unreal to the world of ordinary human conduct. John of Salisbury's faith that something exists not present in the world of human conduct leads him to want a demonstrative science of conduct by which one could argue from principles to unmistakable conclusions. John Locks thinks it is possible to develop a demonstrative science of ethics, believing that we may come to know propositions of conduct so certain that our minds could not doubt them or resist them. And Condillac's "nature" appears to be so undefiled that it could only exist apart from the uncertainties of human conduct. Thus each of them reveals a desire for a kind of certainty which is beyond the province of human conduct.

Their ambiguity, then, lies in (1) exemplifying in their writings a common sense empiricism that is sensitive to the facts in and of human conduct, while (2) espousing a quest for certainty which makes the voice of God, of reason, or of scientifically determined principles the standard to which the facts of human conduct must look in order to find their true places in the nature of things. Yet these writers do not show us demonstrative principles of conduct. Their passion for certainty is ameliorated again and again by the hold which the world of conduct has on them. Ultimately, they do not forsake the search for wisdom by substituting for it the quest for certainty. This is because they are sensitive to the ways of human conduct: they are aware of the evil, the sinning, and the recalcitrance in the world of human conduct. As a consequence of their awareness and sensitivity, they cannot show us the kind of principles they desire. Instead, they settle for the possibility of improved conduct. What they desire is certainty, but what they gain is possibility. They press on in ways which illustrate Aristotle's idea that the actual ends of doing are found in conduct, rather than in principles outside of conduct. They desire what is beyond human conduct; yet in their practical wisdom, what they show us is what Aristotle says they must show us. In their striving for certainty they are forced to settle for something else, the probable, the uncertain, the incomplete.

Ultimately, then, all of our writers on conduct stand against the belief that standards for experience must be erected which will transcend experience. All standards of that sort, when taken as ends of activity, rather than as possible means by which activity takes place, do violence to Aristotle's idea that the starting point of our investigations is "that which is to be," and to Dewey's idea that the ends of activity function *in* activity. Whether or not "that which is to be" in fact, *will* be, is an empirical question whose reply can be determined by the activity in which the starting point functions as a *possible* end of action. As Plato has Socrates say in the *Theaetetus*, whether our ideas are "mere wind-eggs and not worth the rearing,"[3] can be determined only by continuing the investigation, by conducting ourselves in certain ways.

To illustrate ways in which our writers take ends to function in activity as possible means by which the activity might take place, we may point to their attempts to "follow nature." For Aristotle, education aims to fill up "nature's deficiencies." John of Salisbury holds that virtue can be "victorious over nature." For him, nature's ways are "roundabout," while reason's ways are "direct." It is not too much to say that educating Emile is an attempt to make the most of our original nature in a world is which the one who has been corrupted has to go through something akin to Augustine's steps to Wisdom. For Rousseau, our conduct is our own worst enemy, and yet our conduct is the only hope for ameliorating the evil that is always with us. Even Condillac, who comes close to saying that we can literally follow nature, and who sometimes writes as if we "find" our lessons for conduct in nature, then says, "Nature makes laws with us." Rousseau acknowledged, more directly than Condillac was able to do, that we must *make* our nature. And Rousseau agonized over the difficulties in understanding the nature that we are making. The problem is that we are caught up in trying to "follow" that which is being made while that nature is changing. And what is more, the nature that is being made is *our* nature. Each of these thinkers, in his own way, shows us that the nature of our nature is an empirical question, whatever the idea we hold of it as we begin its investigation; and we cannot escape the fact that the way we conduct the investigation is a part of and affects the very nature that we make and come to understand.

Thus understanding our nature is inescapably a part of the activities by which we aim to improve ourselves. Aristotle holds forth some hope for gaining happiness in a polis of a certain kind. The prospect of improving our conduct is restated in the Roman orators, in John of Salisbury, in Locke, Watts, and Condillac, and in Dewey's idea of growth. Yet in Vico and Rousseau there is a sense of the inevitability of the ways in which human limitations stand in the way of bettering the human condition. For Vico and Rousseau, a question about improvement is not a good question. Vico and Rousseau are not at home in a world in which people seek progress. They strive to act in the midst of necessities in things which are destined to take control of human ends. Human integrity is determined, not by whether or not we "make progress," but by the ways in which we learn to make and do without any assurance that our making and doing will change things for better or for worse. We must recall that Aristotle, in his own way, expresses no great confidence that happiness will be gained, in his remark that "one swallow does not make spring." And Dewey, while no fatalist, writes of our inability to command events, calling for us to go on, to be strengthened by the humility we earn as we fail to gain the control which our desires call for. In holding that the theory of education is a theory of conduct, our writers show us that our nature is being made in our strivings to do and to grow. Yet they refuse to guarantee improvement, saying that we are entitled only to the knowledge that we are forced by the nature of things to make ourselves.

Our writers on conduct show us that our ideas are part of the reality of any situation. Our ideas aim to alter the situation for the better just because they are of the situation, rather than apart from it. Whatever comes to be and to be known is conduct of a kind. It is the way of being which has tested the ideas whose origins were in and of the situation. From Aristotle to Dewey, a common idea has endured: the meaning of human nature is found in the conduct of human beings; and the nature of the conduct is the human drama which has been enacted before our very eyes.

Their own writings show us examples of knowing, doing, and making as dramas of human experience. In making human conduct the subject matter of our investigation, we are inescapably enacting these dramas even while we try to investigate them. And that is what education is: knowing, doing, and making in dramas that we have created, and from whose consequences we cannot escape. We grow, we learn, we find new meanings; we become happy and unhappy, we become good and bad; we do all of these things in the contexts of human experience. We cannot escape the limitations and the unknown possibilities in what we have done; we cannot escape the necessity of determining our future possibilities in the dramas of human experience. It is our part to create our own conduct according to all that we have learned in the past, in the context of our present circumstances. This is true education, through which we make our nature.

NOTES

Chapter 1

1. *The Oxford English Dictionary* (Oxford: At the Clarendon Press, 1933), Vol. II, p. 791.

2. *Ibid.,* Vol. I, p. 93.

3. *Ibid.,* Vol. III, p. 563.

4. In the Preface to *The Phenomenology of the Spirit,* translated by Walter Kaufmann, *Hegel: Reinterpretation, Texts, and Commentary* (Garden City: Doubleday & Co., 1965), p. 406.

5. *Two Treatises of Government,* edited by Peter Laslett (New York: Mentor Book, 1965), p. 98.

6. John Dewey, *Experience and Nature* (Chicago: Open Court Publishing Co., 1925), p. 46.

7. Aristotle, *Nicomachean Ethics,* VI. 5. 1140b3–4. Translated by H. Rackham, Loeb Classical Library (Cambridge: Harvard University Press, 1975).

8. John Dewey, *Democracy and Education* (Carbondale: Southern Illinois University Press, 1980), p. 55.

9. Michael Oakeshott, *On Human Conduct* (Oxford: Clarendon Press, 1975).

10. *Ibid.,* p. 32.

11. *Ibid.,* p. 33.

12. *Ibid.*

13. *Ibid.* Preface, p. vii. The three parts of his book are entitled "On the Theoretical Understanding of Human Conduct," "On the Civil Condition," and "On the Character of a Modern European State."

Chapter 2

1. *Nicomachean Ethics,* X. 9. 1179b 21–22. Translated by H. Rackham, Loeb Classical Library (Cambridge: Harvard University Press, 1975).

2. *Nemea.* I. 33–47. Translated by Richmond Lattimore, *The Odes of Pindar,* 2nd ed. (Chicago: University of Chicago Press, 1974).

3. Pierre Riché, *Education and Culture in the Barbarian West, Sixth Through Eighth Centuries.* Translated by John J. Contreni (Columbia: University of South Carolina Press, 1976), p. 10.

4. *The Odes of Pindar. Pythia.* VIII. 95–97.

5. *Ibid. Olympia.* X. 20–21.

6. *Ibid. Olympia.* X. 22–23.

7. *Ibid. Nemea.* III. 70–74.

8. *Ibid. Nemea.* XI. 47–48.

9. *Ibid. Pythia.* III. 103–4.

10. *Ibid. Isthmia.* IV. 32–34.

11. H. I. Marrou, *A History of Education in Antiquity,* translated by George Lamb (New York: New American Library, 1964), p. 31.

12. *The Odes of Pindar. Pythia.* III. 108–9, 114–15. Cf. *Isthmia.* IV. 44–45: "A thing said walks in immortality if it has been said well."

13. *Ibid. Olympia.* I. 115–17.

14. *Ibid. Olympia.* II. 83–85.

15. *Ibid. Olympia.* II. 86–88.

16. *Ibid. Olympia.* IX. 100–104.

17. *Ibid. Olympia.* XI. 19–20.

18. *Ibid. Nemea.* III. 43–52. Achilles and Cheiron were favorite subjects of ancient vase-painters. F. A. G. Beck includes 19 illustrations from vase-paintings showing young Achilles and Cheiron, in *Album of Greek Education: The Greeks at School and Play* (Sydney: Cheiron Press, 1979), pp. 9–12 and Figures 1–19.

19. Homer, *The Iliad.* IX. 436–39. Translated by E. V. Rieu (Baltimore: Penguin Books, 1966), p. 172.

20. *Ibid.* IX. 484–85.

21. Thucydides, *History of the Peloponnesian War,* translated by Rex Warner (Baltimore: Penguin Books, 1954), p. 119.

22. *A History of Education in Antiquity,* p. 33.

23. Aeschylus, *Agamemnon.* 179–82. Translated by Philip Vellacott (Baltimore: Penguin Books, 1956).

24. *Ibid.* 218.

25. *Ibid.* 250–51.

26. Sophocles, *Antigone.* 443–47, 455–58. Translated by H. D. F. Kitto (New York: Oxford University Press, 1964).

27. Euripides, *Hecuba.* 277–86. Translated by William Arrowsmith (Chicago: University of Chicago Press, 1958).

28. *Ibid.* 346–52, 357–61, 366–67, 375–78.

29. *Ibid.* 379–82.

30. *Ibid.* 383–84.

31. *Ibid.* 864-67.

32. *The Poems of Sappho.* Translated by Suzy Q. Groden (Indianapolis: The Library of Liberal Arts, 1986). Poem 29.

33. *Ibid.* Poem 47.

34. *Ibid.* Poem 8.

35. *Ibid.* Poem 5.

36. *Ibid.*

37. *Ibid.* Poem 9.

38. *Ibid.* Poem 32.

39. *History of the Peloponnesian War,* pp. 118–19.

40. *Antidosis.* 166. Translated by George Norlin, Loeb Classical Library (New York: G. P. Putnam's Sons, 1929), *Isocrates,* Vol. II.

41. *Antidosis.* 6–7.

42. *Areopagiticus.* 72–73. Translated by George Norlin, Loeb Classical Library (New York: G. P. Putnam's Sons, 1929), *Isocrates,* Vol. II.

43. *Antidosis.* 186–88.

44. *Antidosis.* 187.

45. *Antidosis.* 277.

46. Plato, *Meno.* 72c, 79d–e. Translated by W. K. C. Guthrie (Baltimore: Penguin Books, 1956), pp. 117, 127.

47. *Ibid.* 80d, p. 128.

48. *Ibid.* 81c–d, pp. 129–30.

49. *Ibid.* 100b, p. 157.

50. Plato, *Laws.* I. 644d. Translated by R. G. Bury, Loeb Classical Library (Cambridge: Harvard University Press, 1952).

51. *Ibid.* VII. 804a–b.

52. *Nicomachean Ethics.* VI. 6. 1140b 3–4.

53. *Ibid.* VI. 6. 1140b 2.

54. Plato, *Republic.* VI. 508e. Translated by F. M. Cornford, *The Republic of Plato.* (New York: Oxford University Press, 1954), p. 220.

55. Plato, *Phaedrus.* X. 247e. Translated by R. Hackforth, *Plato's Phaedrus* (New York: The Liberal Arts Press, 1952), p. 78.

56. *Ibid.* X. 248a–b, p. 79.

Chapter 3

1. Max Fisch's idea is that the one science at work in the *Nicomachean Ethics* and the *Politics* is the "poliscraft"—"the art or craft of creating a polis, keeping it going, guiding it into change for the better, guarding it from change for the worse." See Fisch's "The Poliscraft: A Dialogue,"

in *Philosophy and the Civilizing Arts: Essays Presented to Herbert W. Schneider,* edited by Craig Walton and John P. Anton (Athens: Ohio University Press, 1974), p. 26.

2. *Nicomachean Ethics.* I. 2. 1094a 20–23. Translated by H. Rackham, Loeb Classical Library (Cambridge: Harvard University Press, 1975).

3. *Ibid.* I. 2. 1094a 29.

4. *Ibid.* I. 2. 1094b 6–8.

5. *Ibid.* I. 2. 1094b 5–6.

6. *Ibid.* I. 3. 1094b 19–28.

7. *Ibid.* I. 3. 1095a 3–4.

8. *Ibid.* I. 7. 1097a 16–17.

9. *Ibid.* I. 7. 1097a 17–19.

10. *Ibid.* I. 7. 1097a 34.

11. *Ibid.* I. 7. 1097b 27.

12. *Ibid.* I. 7. 1098a 13–20.

13. *Ibid.* VI. 13. 1144b 27–28.

14. *Ibid.* I. 4. 1095b 2–3.

15. *Ibid.* I. 4. 1095b 4–7.

16. *Ibid.* I. 7. 1098b 2–3.

17. *Ibid.* I. 8. 1098b 10–12.

18. *Ibid.* I. 7. 1098b 7–8.

19. *Ibid.* II. 1. 1103a 14–17.

20. *Ibid.* II. 1. 1103a 24–27.

21. *Ibid.* II. 1. 1103a 28–29.

22. *Ibid.* II. 1. 1103b 1–2.

23. *Ibid.* I. 9. 1100a 2–5.

24. *Ibid.* II. 6. 1106b 35. Cf. *Eudemian Ethics.* VII. 4. 1239b 11–12.

25. *Ibid.* II. 6. 1106b 36 – 1107a 2.

26. *Ibid.* II. 2. 1103b 27–31.

27. *Ibid.* VI. 3. 1139b 15–17.

28. *Ibid.* VI. 3. 1139b 23.

29. *Ibid.* VI. 3. 1139b 31.

30. *Ibid.* VI. 4. 1140a 1–2.

31. *Ibid.* VI. 4. 1140a 12–18.

32. *Ibid.* VI. 5. 1140b 3–5.

33. *Ibid.* VI. 6. 1140b 34–35 – 1141a 1–2.

34. *Ibid.* VI. 5. 1140a 26–31.

35. *Ibid.* VI. 5. 1140b 1–2.

36. *Politics.* I. 1. 1252a 24–26. Translated by H. Rackham, Loeb Classical Library (Cambridge: Harvard University Press, 1944).

37. *Ibid.* I. 1. 1252a 26 – 1252b 29.

38. *Ibid.* I. 1. 1252b 29–32.

39. *Ibid.* I. 1. 1252b 33–34.

40. *Ibid.* I. 1. 1253a 3–4.

41. *Ibid.* I. 5. 1260a 14.

42. *Ibid.* I. 5. 1260a 32–34.

43. *Nicomachean Ethics.* III. 12. 1119b 13–15.

44. *On the Parts of Animals.* I. 1. 639b 15–16. Translated by William Ogle, *The Basic Works of Aristotle,* edited by Richard McKeon (New York: Random House, 1941).

45. *On the Parts of Animals.* I. 1. 640a 4.

46. *Eudemian Ethics.* II. 11. 1227b 33–34. Translated by H. Rackham, Loeb Classical Library (Cambridge: Harvard University Press, 1971).

47. *Politics.* VII. 15. 1337a 1–2.

48. *Ibid.* VII. 13. 1334b 10.

49. *Ibid.* VII. 13. 1334b 11–13.

50. *Ibid.* VII. 13. 1334b 16–18.

51. *Ibid.* VII. 15. 1136a 25–28.

52. *Ibid.* VII. 15. 1336a 30–31.

Chapter 4

1. *De Oratore.* II. xxii. 94. Translated by E. W. Sutton and H. Rackham, Loeb Classical Library (Cambridge: Harvard University Press, 1967).

2. *Ibid.* I. xxviii. 128.

3. *Ibid.*

4. *Ibid.* I. xxvii. 123. Cf. I. xxvi. 120: "The better the orator, the more profoundly is he frightened of the difficulty of speaking, and of the doubtful fate of a speech, and of the anticipations of an audience."

5. *Agamemnon.* 179. Translated by Philip Vellacott. *The Oresteian Trilogy* (Baltimore: Penguin Books, 1967), p. 48.

6. *De Oratore.* III. xv. 57. Translated by H. Rackham, Loeb Classical Library (Cambridge: Harvard University Press, 1968).

7. *Ibid.*

8. *Ibid.* III. xxxiv. 141.

9. *Ibid.*

10. *Ibid.* III. xxxv. 142.

11. *Ibid.* III. xxxv. 143.

12. *Ibid.*

13. *Ibid.* III. xvi. 60.

14. *Ibid.* III. xvi. 61.

15. *Ibid.* III. xiv. 54–55.

16. *Ibid.* III. xiv. 55.

17. *Ibid.* III. xvi. 56.

18. *Ibid.* III. xvii. 64. Cf. I. xii. 60. There Cicero insists that an orator must make "a most careful search into all those theories respecting the natural characters and the habits and conduct of mankind."

19. *Nicomachean Ethics.* VI. 4. 1140a1–2.

20. *De Oratore.* III. xix. 72.

21. *Ibid.* III. xix. 73.

22. *Ibid.* III. xxi. 80.

23. *Nicomachean Ethics.* VI. 5. 1140b4–5.

24. *De Oratore.* I. iii. 12.

25. *Ibid.*

26. *Ibid.* II. xxxvi. 152.

27. For Aristotle, what is "knowable in itself" comes, if at all, at the end of our investigations. At the beginning of our investigations, however, we must make do with what is "known to us," which is known as a consequence of our history together. It is what we know because of our experience in common. See *Nicomachean Ethics.* I. 4. 1095b2–3.

28. *De Oratore.* I. vi. 20.

29. *Ibid.* I. xxiii. 108.

30. For Aristotle, scientific knowledge is demonstrative knowledge, whose objects exist by necessity, rather than by human action. *Nicomachean Ethics.* VI. 3. 1139b23, 31.

31. *De Oratore.* II. xxx. 131.

32. *Cooperating* emphasizes the need for deliberately principled conduct, rather than conduct which might "happen" to conform to principle. See *Nicomachean Ethics.* VI. 13. 1144b27–28.

33. *De Oratore.* I. xxv. 114.

34. *Ibid.* I. xxv. 115.

35. See Plato's *Meno,* 99e, 100b.

36. *De Oratore.* I. xxv. 115.

37. *Ibid.* I. xxxiii. 151.

38. *Ibid.* I. xxxii. 146–47.

39. *Ibid.* I. xxxii. 146.

40. *Ibid.* I. xxvi. 120, and I. xxvi. 123.

41. Plato's *Phaedrus,* 248a–b.

42. *Nicomachean Ethics.* I. 7. 1098a13–20.

43. Quintilian's *Institutes of Oratory.* I. vi. 1–3. Translated by John Selby Watson (London: George Bell and Sons, 1875).

44. *Ibid.* Preface. 9. Cf. XII. ii. 1.

45. *Ibid.* I. vi. 45.

46. *Ibid.* II. iii. 12.

47. *Ibid.* I. i. 4–5.

48. *Ibid.* XII. i. 25.

49. *Ibid.* XII. i. 27.

50. *Ibid.*

51. *Ibid.* XII. ii. 17.

52. *Ibid.* XII. ii. 27.

53. *Ibid.* XII. ii. 29.

54. *Ibid.* II. xvii. 39.

55. *Ibid.* XII. xi. 30.

56. *Ibid.*

57. *Ibid.* II. xv. 3–14.

58. *Ibid.* II. xv. 6.

59. *Ibid.* II. xv. 38.

60. *Ibid.*

61. *Ibid.* II. xvi. 11.

62. *Ibid.* II. xiv. 4.

63. *Ibid.* II. xvii. 25.

64. *Ibid.* II. xviii. 2.

65. *Ibid.* II. xviii. 4.

66. *Ibid.* II. xviii. 5.

67. *Ibid.*

68. *Ibid.* II. xviii. 2.

69. Stanley F. Bonner, in the Preface to his *Education in Ancient Rome* (Berkeley: University of California Press, 1977), acknowledges a special indebtedness to Quintilian. And in a chapter called "Learning the Art of the Advocate," Quintilian's *Institutes* is mentioned in 112 of 142 notes.

70. *Institutes of Oratory.* II. xviii. 2.

71. *Ibid.* II. xx. 4.

72. *Ibid.* II. xx. 9.

Chapter 5

1. Werner Jaeger's *Paideia: The Ideals of Greek Culture,* Vol. I. Translated by Gilbert Highet (New York: Oxford University Press, 1945), is an incomparable study of its subject. In the Preface, Jaeger calls paideia "the shaping of the Greek Character".

2. H. I. Marrou, *A History of Education in Antiquity.* Translated by George Lamb (Madison: University of Wisconsin Press, 1982), p. 99.

3. See William Ralph Inge, *The Philosophy of Plotinus,* Vol. I (New York: Longmans, Green, 1929), Third Edition, p. 99. "In Philo, though God sends his 'Powers' into the world, the world is always outside God, and as such deprived of value."

4. Samuel Sandmel, *Philo of Alexandria: An Introduction* (New York: Oxford University Press, 1979), p. 17.

5. *Ibid.*

6. Philo, *On Mating with the Preliminary Studies.* 9. Translated by F. H. Colson and G. H. Whitaker, *Philo,* Vol. IV (Cambridge: Harvard University Press, 1949).

7. *Ibid.,* 180.

8. *Ibid.,* 126.

9. *Ibid.,* 166.

10. *Ibid.,* 79.

11. Philo, *On Flight and Finding.* 138. Translated by F. H. Colson and G. H. Whitaker, *Philo,* Vol. V (Cambridge: Harvard University Press, 1949).

12. *Ibid.*

13. *Ibid.,* 169.

14. *Ibid.,* 153.

15. *Ibid.,* 165.

16. Philo, *Every Good Man Is Free.* 116. Translated by F. H. Colson, *Philo,* Vol. IX (Cambridge: Harvard University Press, 1941).

17. *Ibid.,* 27.

18. *Ibid.,* 88.

19. *Ibid.,* 96.

20. *Ibid.,* 109.

21. Werner Jaeger, *Early Christianity and Greek Paideia* (New York: Oxford University Press, 1961), p. 134 n. 33.

22. *Laws.* X. 897b. Translated by Jaeger in *Early Christianity and Greek Paideia,* p. 133 n. 29.

23. Clement's *Paedagogus.* 1. 5. 12. Translated by Simon P. Wood as *Christ the Educator* (New York: Fathers of the Church, 1954).

24. *Ibid.* 1. 5. 14.

25. *Ibid.*

26. *Ibid.* 1. 5. 15.

27. *Ibid.*

28. *Ibid.* 1. 5. 14.

29. *Ibid.*

30. *Ibid.* 1. 5. 17.

31. *Ibid.*

32. *Ibid.* 1. 5. 14.

33. Matthew. 18. 3. Quoted in *ibid.* 1. 5. 12.

34. *Ibid.* 1. 5. 13.

35. Matthew. 19. 14. Quoted in *ibid.* 1. 5. 12.

36. *Ibid.* 1. 5. 16.

37. *Ibid.*

38. *Ibid.* 1. 5. 17.

39. *Ibid.* 1. 5. 19.

40. *Ibid.* Quoting Romans. 16. 19.

41. *Ibid.*

42. *Ibid.*

43. *Ibid.* 1. 5. 17.

44. *Ibid.* 1. 5. 16.

45. *Ibid.* 1. 6. 32.

46. *Ibid.*

47. Augustine, *The City of God.* II. 7. Translated by Henry Bettenson (Baltimore: Pelican Books, 1972).

48. *Ibid.*

49. *Ibid.*

50. *Ibid.* VIII. 5.

51. *Ibid.*

52. *Ibid.* VIII. 8.

53. *Ibid.* VIII. 4.

54. Augustine, *On Christian Doctrine.* II. vii. 9–11. Translated by D. W. Robertson, Jr. (Indianapolis: Liberal Arts Press, 1958).

55. *Ibid.* II. vii. 9.

56. *Ibid.*

57. *Ibid.* II. vii. 10.

58. *Ibid.*

59. *Ibid.* II. vii. 11.

60. *Ibid.*

61. *Ibid.*

62. *Ibid.*

63. *The City of God.* XXII. 22.

64. *Ibid.*

65. *Ibid.*

66. Augustine, *The Confessions.* I. xii. 19. Translated by E. B. Pusey (London: J. M. Dent & Sons, 1907).

67. *Ibid.* I. vii. 11.

68. *Ibid.*

69. *Ibid.* I. ix. 14.

70. *Ibid.* I. xii. 19.

71. *The City of God.* XXII. 22.

72. *The Confessions.* I. xviii. 30.

73. Matthew. 19. 14. Quoted in Clement's *Christ the Educator.* I. 5. 12.

74. *Christ the Educator.* 1. 5. 14.

75. *The Confessions.* I. xviii. 30.

76. Philip Schaff, editor. *A Select Library of the Nicene and Post-Nicene Fathers of the Christian Church.* Volume V: *Saint Augustine: Anti-Pelagian Writings* (New York: The Christian Literature Co., 1887), p. xv, in "Introductory Essay on Augustine and the Pelagian Controversy," by B. B. Warfield.

77. *Ibid.,* p. xv n. 7.

78. *Ibid.* "On the Merits and Forgiveness of Sins, and On the Baptism of Infants." I. 66. Translated by Peter Holmes.

79. *Ibid.* I. 67.

80. *Ibid.*

81. *Ibid.* I. 65.

82. *The Confessions.* I. xviii. 31.

83. *Ibid.*

84. *Ibid.*

85. *Ibid.*

Chapter 6

1. *The Metalogicon of John of Salisbury.* Prologue. Translated by Daniel D. McGarry (Gloucester, Mass.: Peter Smith, 1971).

2. *Ibid.* I. 8.

3. *Ibid.*

4. *Ibid.*

5. *Ibid.* III. Prologue.

6. *Ibid.* I. 9.

7. *Ibid.* I. 10.

8. *Ibid.*

9. *Ibid.*

10. *Ibid.* I. 11.

11. *Ibid.*

12. *Ibid.* Cf. *Ibid.* I. 14.

13. *Ibid.* I. 11.

14. *Physics.* II. 8. 199a16–17. Translated by R. P. Hardie and R. K. Gaye, *The Basic Works of Aristotle,* edited by Richard McKeon (New York: Random House, 1941).

15. *The Metalogicon.* I. 14.

16. *Ibid.* I. 17.

17. *Ibid.*

18. *Ibid.*

19. *Ibid.* I. 16.

20. *Ibid.*

21. *Ibid.*

22. *Ibid.* I. 22.

23. *Ibid.*

24. *Ibid.*

25. *Ibid.*

26. *Ibid.* I. 23.

27. *Ibid.*

28. *Ibid.*

29. *Ibid.*

30. *Ibid.* II. 1.

31. *Ibid.* II. 2.

32. *Ibid.* II. 3.

33. *Ibid.*

34. *Ibid.*

35. *Ibid.*

36. *Ibid.*

37. *Ibid.* II. 4.

38. *Ibid.*

39. *Ibid.*

40. *Ibid.*

41. *Ibid.* II. 5.

42. *Ibid.* II. 9.

43. *Ibid.* II. 10.

44. *Ibid.* II. 9.

45. *Ibid.* IV. 12.

46. *Ibid.*

47. *Ibid.*

48. *Ibid.*

49. *Ibid.*

50. *Ibid.*

51. *Ibid.* IV. 13.

52. *Ibid.*

53. *Ibid.*

54. *Ibid.*

55. *Ibid.*

56. *Ibid.* IV. 14. Words in brackets added by translator.

57. *Ibid.*

58. *Ibid.* IV. 16.

59. *Ibid.*

Chapter 7

1. John Locke, *An Essay Concerning Human Understanding,* edited by John W. Yolton (London: J. M. Dent & Sons, 1961), Book II, Chapter I, Section 2. Hereafter this will be referred to as *Essay.*

2. *Essay.* IV. i. 2.

3. *Ibid.* IV. i. 4.

4. *Ibid.* IV. ii. 1.

5. *Ibid.*

6. *Ibid.*

7. *Ibid.* IV. ii. 7.

8. Cf. *ibid.* IV. iii. 26.

9. Morton White, *Science and Sentiment in America* (New York: Oxford University Press, 1972), p. 12.

10. *Essay.* IV. iii. 18. Cf. *ibid.* IV. iv. 7 and IV. xii. 8.

11. *Essay.* IV. iii. 18.

12. *Ibid.*

13. II. ii. 4. *Two Treatises of Government,* edited by Peter Laslett (New York: Mentor Books, 1965). My emphasis.

14. *Essay.* IV. xiv. 1.

15. *Ibid.* IV. xiv. 2.

16. *Ibid.* IV. xiv. 3.

17. Strictly speaking, Locke calls *judgment* that faculty of the mind which is exercised immediately about things, and calls *assent* or *dissent* that faculty which is exercised about truth-claims delivered in words. We are using the term *judgment* to stand for activity of the mind which gains probability, whether about things or words.

18. *Essay.* IV. xv. 1.

19. *Ibid.* IV. xxi. 3.

20. Peter Gay, *John Locke on Education* (New York: Teachers College, Columbia University, 1964), p. 1.

21. John W. Yolton, *John Locke and Education* (New York: Random House, 1971), p. 9.

22. *Ibid.*, pp. 9–10.

23. *Ibid.*, p. 10.

24. *Ibid.*, pp. 10–11.

25. *Two Treatises of Government,* p. 98.

26. *Ibid.*, p. 100.

27. *Ibid.*, p. 101.

28. See especially *Some Thoughts Concerning Education,* Sec. 66.

29. *Ibid.* Sec. 69.

30. *Ibid.* Sec. 135.

31. *Ibid.* Sec. 140.

32. *Ibid.* Sec. 81.

33. *Ibid.*

34. John Locke, *Of the Conduct of the Understanding.* Sec. 1. Edited by Francis W. Garforth (New York: Teachers College Press, 1966). My emphasis.

35. *Ibid.* Sec. 4.

36. *Ibid.*

37. *Ibid.* Cf. *Some Thoughts Concerning Education,* Sec. 1, where he writes, "I think I may say, that, of all the men we meet with, nine parts of ten are what they are, good or evil, useful or not, by their education."

38. *Essay.* IV. xviii. 2.

39. *Ibid.* IV. xviii. 4.

40. *Ibid.* IV. xviii. 7.

41. *Ibid.*

42. *Ibid.* IV. xviii. 8.

43. *Ibid.* IV. xviii. 9.

44. *The Reasonableness of Christianity as Delivered in the Scriptures,* in *The Works of John Locke,* Ninth Edition, Volume 6 (London: Printed for T. Longman etc., 1794), pp. 139–40.

45. *Ibid.,* p. 139.

46. *Ibid.,* p. 140.

47. *Ibid.,* p. 143.

48. *Of the Conduct of the Understanding.* Sec. 43.

49. *The Works of the Late Reverend and Learned Isaac Watts* (London: Printed for T. and T. Longmans, etc., 1753), Volume V, p. 1.

50. *Ibid.*

51. *Ibid.,* p. 3.

52. *Ibid.,* p. 4.

53. *Ibid.,* pp. 168–69.

54. *Ibid.,* p. 168.

55. *Ibid.,* p. 169.

56. *Ibid.,* p. 90.

57. *Ibid.,* p. 87.

58. *Ibid.*

59. *The Improvement of the Mind, or, A Supplement to the Art of Logic,* etc. (New Brunswick: Printed by Lewis Deare, 1813), p. 258.

60. *Ibid.,* p. 174.

61. *Ibid.,* p. 175.

62. *Ibid.,* p. 257.

63. *Works of . . . Isaac Watts,* Volume V, pp. 364–65.

Chapter 8

1. Giambattista Vico, *On the Study Methods of our Time,* translated by Elio Gianturco (Indianapolis: Bobbs-Merrill Co., 1965), p. 35.

2. *Ibid.,* p. 13.

3. *Ibid.*

4. *Ibid.,* p. 19.

5. *Ibid.*

6. *Ibid.,* p. 14.

7. *Ibid.,* p. 41.

8. *Ibid.,* p. 13.

9. *Ibid.,* p. 17.

10. *Ibid.,* p. 25.

11. *Ibid.,* p. 3.

12. *Ibid.*

13. *Ibid.,* p. 35.

14. *Ibid.,* p. 43.

15. *Ibid.*

16. *Ibid.*

17. *Ibid.*

18. Max H. Fisch cites this expression of Vico in his Introduction to *The Autobiography of Giambattista Vico,* translated by Thomas Goddard Bergin and Max Harold Fisch (Ithaca, New York: Cornell University Press, Great Seal Books, 1963), p. 60.

19. *On the Study Methods of our Time,* p. 23.

20. *Ibid.*

21. *The New Science of Giambattista Vico,* Revised translation of the Third Edition (1744), by Thomas Goddard Bergin and Max Harold Fisch (Ithaca, New York: Cornell University Press, 1968), 34. (The numbers cited in reference to the *New Science* are to paragraphs in the work.)

22. *Ibid.,* 331.

23. *Ibid.,* 147.

24. *Ibid.,* 314.

25. *Ibid.,* 367.

26. *Ibid.,* 120.

27. *Ibid.*, 122.

28. *Ibid.*, 816.

29. *Ibid.*, 374, 375.

30. *Ibid.*, 400.

31. *Ibid.*, 375.

32. *Ibid.*, 383.

33. *Ibid.*, 363.

34. *Ibid.*, 405.

35. *Ibid.*, 819.

36. *Ibid.*, 821.

37. *Ibid.*, 819.

38. *Ibid.*, 127.

39. *Ibid.*, 215–19.

40. *Ibid.*, 1108.

Chapter 9

1. Jean-Jacques Rousseau, *The Social Contract* and *Discourse on the Origin and Foundation of Inequality Among Mankind,* edited by Lester G. Crocker (New York: Washington Square Press, 1967).

2. Jean-Jacques Rousseau, *Emile* or *On Education,* translated by Allan Bloom (New York: Basic Books, 1979).

3. *Discourse,* p. 177.

4. *Ibid.*, p. 173.

5. *Emile,* p. 34.

6. *Discourse,* pp. 167–68.

7. *Ibid.*, p. 171.

8. *Ibid.*, p. 175.

9. *Ibid.*, p. 219.

10. *Ibid.*, pp. 219–220.

11. *Ibid.,* p. 244. My emphasis.

12. *Ibid.,* p. 177.

13. *Ibid.,* pp. 171–172.

14. *Ibid.,* p. 245.

15. *Ibid.*

16. *Ibid.,* p. 173.

17. *Ibid.,* p. 188.

18. *Ibid.*

19. *Emile,* pp. 39, 40.

20. *Ibid.,* pp. 41–42.

21. *Ibid.,* p. 90.

22. *Ibid.,* p. 107.

23. *Ibid.,* p. 108.

24. *Ibid.,* p. 167.

25. *Ibid.,* p. 178.

26. *Ibid.,* p. 205.

27. *Ibid.,* p. 93.

28. *Ibid.,* p. 339.

29. *Ibid.,* p. 408.

30. *Ibid.,* p. 63.

31. *Ibid.,* p. 158.

32. *Ibid.,* p. 162.

33. *Ibid.,* p. 472.

34. *Ibid.,* p. 235.

35. *Ibid.,* p. 461.

36. *Ibid.,* p. 473.

37. *Ibid.,* p. 471.

38. *Ibid.,* p. 446.

39. *Ibid.,* p. 473.

40. *Ibid.,* p. 112n.

41. *Ibid.,* p. 472.

42. *Ibid.,* p. 473.

43. *Ibid.*

44. *Ibid.,* p. 473.

Chapter 10

1. In J. J. Chambliss, *The Origins of American Philosophy of Education* (The Hague: Martinus Nijhoff, 1968), several nineteenth century writers, including Joseph Neef, George Jardine, James G. Carter, and Thomas Tate, are seen to have advocated an "inductive empiricism" which tried to base educational theory on an empirical method that would constitute rational conduct. Among these, only Neef, the translator of Condillac's *Logic,* was directly influenced by Condillac's writings; yet the similarities among them are sufficient to show us that Condillac-like ideas, whatever their origins, were well-known among educational theorists in the nineteenth century.

2. Isabel F. Knight, *The Geometric Spirit: The Abbe de Condillac and the French Enlightenment* (New Haven: Yale University Press, 1968), p. 14.

3. Etienne Bonnot de Condillac, *The Logic of Condillac.* Translated by Joseph Neef, as an Illustration of the Plan of Education Established at his School near Philadelphia (Philadelphia: [By the translator], printed 1809), p. 3. Hereafter this will be referred to as *Logic.*

4. *Ibid.*

5. *Ibid.,* p. 6.

6. *Ibid.,* p. 9.

7. *Ibid.,* p. 16.

8. *An Essay on the Origin of Human Knowledge, Being a Supplement to Mr. Locke's Essay on the Human Understanding,* translated from the French of the Abbé de Condillac, by [Thomas] Nugent (London: Printed for J. Nourse, etc., 1756), pp. 335–36. Hereafter this will be referred to as *Essay.*

9. *Ibid.,* p. 336.

10. *Ibid.*, p. 337. My emphasis.

11. *Ibid.*, pp. 5–6.

12. *Ibid.*, p. 73.

13. *Essay Concerning Human Understanding.* IV. xxi. 3.

14. Condillac's *Essay*, p. 2.

15. *Logic*, p. 40.

16. *Ibid.*

17. *Ibid.*

18. *Ibid.*, p. 41. My emphasis.

19. *Ibid.*, p. 75.

20. *Essay*, p. 315.

21. *Ibid.*, p. 316.

22. *Ibid.*

23. *Ibid.*

24. *Logic*, p. 41.

Chapter 11

1. John Dewey, *Democracy and Education* (Carbondale: Southern Illinois University Press, 1980), p. 338.

2. *Ibid.*, p. 342.

3. *Ibid.*, p. 7.

4. "John Dewey's Social Philosophy," in *New Studies in the Philosophy of John Dewey*, edited by Steven M. Cahn (Hanover, N. H.: University Press of New England, 1977), p. 6.

5. *Democracy and Education*, p. 367.

6. *Ibid.*, p. 368.

7. "John Dewey's Social Philosophy," p. 5.

8. *Democracy and Education*, p. 368.

9. John Dewey, *Human Nature and Conduct* (New York: The Modern Library, 1957), p. 5.

10. *Ibid.,* p. 253.

11. *Ibid.,* p. 201.

12. *Ibid.,* p. 287.

13. *Ibid.,* p. 201.

14. *Ibid.,* p. 210.

15. *Ibid.,* p. 209.

16. *Nicomachean Ethics.* II. 2. 1103b 29.

17. *Democracy and Education,* p. 167.

18. *Ibid.*

19. *Nicomachean Ethics.* II. 2. 1103b 30.

20. John Dewey, "The Postulate of Immediate Empiricism," *Journal of Philosophy, Psychology, and Scientific Methods,* II (July 20, 1905), p. 393.

21. *Ibid.*

22. *Democracy and Education,* p. 369.

23. *Ibid.*

24. *Human Nature and Conduct,* p. 284.

25. *Ibid.,* p. 285.

26. *Ibid.*

27. *Ibid.,* p. 286.

28. *Democracy and Education,* p. 284.

29. *Human Nature and Conduct,* p. 288.

30. *Ibid.*

31. *Ibid.*

32. *Ibid.,* p. 86.

33. *Ibid.,* p. 21.

34. *Ibid.,* p. 266.

35. *Ibid.,* p. 267.

36. *Ibid.*

Chapter 12

1. Alasdair MacIntyre, *After Virtue* (Notre Dame, Indiana: University of Notre Dame Press, 1981), p. 56.

2. *Nicomachean Ethics.* I. 7. 1097b 27.

3. Plato, *Theaetetus,* 210b. Translated by Francis M. Cornford, *Plato's Theory of Knowledge* (New York: The Liberal Arts Press, 1957), p. 163.

BIBLIOGRAPHIC NOTE _____

The works cited in the essay constitute its essential bibliography. Of course an extensive bibliography exists beyond the most essential materials. A large body of literature exists for some of our authors: Plato, Aristotle, Augustine, Locke, Rousseau, and Dewey; writings on the work of Isocrates, Cicero, Quintilian, Philo, Clement, John of Salisbury, Vico, and Condillac are less extensive. By limiting the scope of this bibliographic note to the sources to which our own work is most indebted, we aim to be selective rather than comprehensive.

C. M. Bowra's *The Greek Experience* (Cleveland: World Publishing Co., 1957) portrays the sense in which the ancient Greek as artist-craftsman-citizen emphasizes the integrity of making and doing in a social context. For a discussion of Homer, Pindar, the sophists, and the tragic poets, which treats ancient Greek culture as the context in which educational questions arose, see Werner Jaeger, *Paideia: the Ideals of Greek Culture*, Vol. I, Second Edition, translated by Gilbert Highet (New York: Oxford University Press, 1945). Walter Kaufmann, in *Tragedy and Philosophy* (Garden City, N.Y.: Anchor Books, 1969), offers the argument that the tragic poets were wiser than they appear in philosophers' criticisms of them. Volume II of Jaeger's *Paideia* contains an insightful discussion of Plato's educational dialogues. And in volume III, Jaeger considers Isocrates' rhetoric to be a cultural ideal.

A comprehensive work on Plato's place in the Western philosophic tradition is A. E. Taylor, *Plato: The Man and His Work* (Cleveland: World Publishing, Co., 1963). In John Herman Randall, Jr., *Plato: Dramatist of the Life of Reason* (New York: Columbia University Press, 1970), Plato's work is taken more for its dramatic and suggestive character than for its systematic philosophy. Plato and Isocrates are called "the masters of the classical tradition" in chapters VI and VII of H. I. Marrou's *A History of Education in Antiquity* (Madison: University of Wisconsin Press, 1982). A systematic treatment of Aristotle's writings is W. D. Ross, *Aristotle: A Complete Exposition of His Works and Thought* (Cleveland: World Publishing Co., 1962). John Herman Randall, Jr., in *Aristotle* (New York: Columbia University Press, 1962), conveys a sense of Aristotle working at knowing. Werner Jaeger's *Aristotle: Fundamentals of the History of His Development*, Second Edition, translated by Richard Robinson (London: Oxford University Press, 1962) is a classic work on the development of Aristotle's thought. Larry Arnhart, in *Aristotle on Political Reasoning: A Commentary on the "Rhetoric"* (DeKalb: Northern Illinois University Press, 1985), provides an argument for the idea that for Aristotle, rhetoric was a serious form of rational discourse, not mere sophistry.

Excellent discussions of the rhetorical tradition in Homer are to be found in Marrou's history, Part III, chapters 5 and 6, as well as in Stanley F. Bonner, *Education in Ancient Rome* (Berkeley: University of California Press, 1977), chapters VI and VII. See also Aubrey Gwynn, *Roman Education from Cicero to Quintilian* (Oxford: Clarendon Press, 1926). For an interesting discussion of the idea that rhetoric is a virtue, see Alan Brinton, "Quintilian, Plato, and the *Vir Bonus*," *Philosophy and Rhetoric*, XVI (No. 3, 1983), 167-184.

One of the best accounts of Augustine's philosophy is Frederick Copleston's *A History of Philosophy*, Vol. II, *Medieval Philosophy*, Part I, *Augustine to Bonaventure* (Garden City, N. Y.: Image Books, 1962), chapters III-VIII. See also Etienne Gilson, *History of Christian Philosophy in the Middle Ages* (New York: Random House, 1955), pp. 70-81. A valuable volume of essays is *Augustine: His Age, Life, and Thought* (New York: Meridian Books, 1957). See especially the essays by Christopher Dawson, "St. Augustine and His Age," and by John-Baptist Reeves, "St. Augustine and Humanism." Gilson's *History* also has an excellent section on Clement of Alexandria, pp. 29-35. Werner Jaeger's discussion of Clement's conception of paideia is to be found in *Early Christianity and Greek Paideia* (New York: Oxford University Press, 1977), pp. 45, 46-47, 54-62, 133n, 29. On Philo's Hellenistic intellectual context and his contributions to various religious points of view, see Harry A. Wolfson, *Philo: Foundations of Religious Philosophy in Judaism, Christianity, and Islam*, 2 volumes (Cambridge:

Harvard University Press, 1947). In William Ralph Inge, *The Philosophy of Plotinus*, Third Edition, Vol. I (New York: Longmans, Green, 1929), pp. 97-99, Philo is treated as one of Plotinus' forerunners. See also Frederick Copleston, *A History of Philosophy*, Vol. I, *Greece and Rome*, Part II (Garden City, N. Y.: Image Books, 1962), pp. 201-206, for a useful account of Philo's philosophy.

Gilson's *History*, pp. 150-53, gives a good brief account of John of Salisbury's philosophy. John's place in educational history is well treated by James Bowen in *A History of Western Education*, Vol. II, *Civilization of Europe, Sixth to Sixteenth Century* (New York: St. Martin's Press, 1975), pp. 79-87.

To supplement Locke's *Essay Concerning Human Understanding* and the writings on education and religion cited in our essay, Locke's Second *Treatise of Government* is especially valuable for studying his thinking on conduct. The edition of Peter Laslett, *Two Treatises of Government* (New York: Mentor Books, 1965), has an insightful introduction to Locke's thought and character. John W. Yolton's *John Locke and Education* (New York: Random House, 1971) is perhaps the best work on the subject in English. A fine essay is Kenneth D. Benne's "The Gentleman: Locke," in Nash, Kazamias, and Perkinson, editors, *The Educated Man: Studies in the History of Educational Thought* (New York: John Wiley & Sons, 1965), pp. 191-223. See John Herman Randall, Jr., *The Career of Philosophy*, Vol. I, *From the Middle Ages to the Enlightenment* (New York: Columbia University Press, 1962), pp. 595-617, for Locke's conception of knowledge.

Max Fisch's Introduction to *The Autobiography of Giambattista Vico*, translated by Max H. Fisch and Thomas G. Bergin (Ithaca: Cornell University Press, 1963), is perhaps the best introduction to Vico's thought and character in English. To see something of the scope and suggestiveness of Vico's work, two collections of essays are valuable. The first is *Giambattista Vico: An International Symposium*, edited by Giorgio Tagliacozzo and Hayden White (Baltimore: Johns Hopkins University Press, 1969). The second, edited by Tagliacozzo and Donald Philip Verene, is *Giambattista Vico's Science of Humanity* (Baltimore: Johns Hopkins University Press, 1976). For a study of Vico's "imaginative universal" and its place in philosophical investigation, see Verene's work, *Vico's Science of Imagination* (Ithaca: Cornell University Press, 1981).

In Peter Gay's *The Enlightenment*, Vol. II, *The Science of Freedom* (New York: Alfred A. Knopf, 1969), pp. 529-552, there is a valuable discussion of Rousseau's place in the Enlightenment. See "The Supposed Primitivism of Rousseau's *Discourse on Inequality*," in Arthur O. Lovejoy, *Essays in the History of Ideas* (New York: G. P. Putnam's, 1960) for an argument against the idea that Rousseau's favorite condition of human beings was the "original" or "most savage" condition. Charles Frankel's introduction to *The Social Contract* (New York: Hafner Publishing Co., 1974) is a useful statement on the relationship between *Emile* and *The Social Contract*. The Summer 1978 issue of *Daedalus* (Vol. 107) is devoted to several studies of Rousseau; the essays by Wokler, Barber, Kesser, Schwartz, and Baczko are especially recommended. For insightful studies of Rousseau's writings in their moral, pedagogical, and literary dimensions see Madeleine B. Ellis, *Julie or La Nouvelle Heloise* (Toronto: University of Toronto Press, 1949), and *Rousseau's Socratic Aemilian Myths* (Columbus: Ohio State University Press, 1977). In the latter, Rousseau's sensitivity to Plato's writings is portrayed in a compelling way.

An excellent work which places Condillac in the context of Enlightenment thinking is Isabel Knight's *The Geometric Spirit: The Abbe de Condillac and the French Enlightenment* (New Haven: Yale University Press, 1968). Knight includes a chapter on Condillac's educational ideas. Nicholas J. Kagdis examines the multi-volumed *Cours D'Etudes*, composed by Condillac for use in tutoring the Prince of Parma, in an unpublished doctoral dissertation at Rutgers University, 1984, entitled *Etienne Bonnot de Condillac's Cours D'Etudes: Analysis and Implications*. Also recommended are pp. 926-931 in Randall's *Career of Philosophy*.

James Gouinlock's *John Dewey's Philosophy of Value* (New York: Humanities Press, 1972) is a first-rate exposition of its subject. Herbert W. Schneider and Darnell Rucker provide an informative introduction to Dewey's ethical writings from 1887-1948, in "Dewey's Ethics," in Jo Ann Boydston, editor, *Guide to the Works of John Dewey* (Carbondale: Southern Illinois University Press, 1970), pp. 99-130. Sidney Hook's Introduction to "The Middle Years" edition of *Democracy and Education* (Carbondale: Southern Illinois University Press, 1980) is a good critical piece. For an example of Dewey's educational theory in action, see the account of the Laboratory School at the University of Chicago, 1896-1903, by Katherine Camp Mayhew and Anna Camp Edwards, *The Dewey School* (New York: D. Appleton-Century, 1936). The influence of Dewey's ideas on community education is found in Elsie Ripley Clapp, *The Use of Resources in Education* (New York: Harper & Brothers, 1952).

INDEX